World Jewry owes a deep debt of gratitude to our colleague, Dr. Manfred Gerstenfeld. Manfred is a noted and respected economist who combines a keen analytical mind with a passion to expose the truth and helps us all understand the world's oldest hatred.

—Rabbi Marvin Hier
Founder and Dean Simon Wiesenthal Center

Demonizing Israel and the Jews, *edited by noted authority Manfred Gerstenfeld, is a remarkable, and indispensable, handbook tracking the world-wide revival of anti-Semitism. The book's interviews with outstanding scholars and specialists succinctly analyze religious, nationalistic/ethnic, and "anti-Zionist" anti-Semitism, from the Arab world to Europe and North America. This is an authoritative, up-to-date guide to the crucial cultural-ideological war—paralleling and reinforcing the political and military-terrorist campaign—being waged in the media, on the web, on campuses, and in international fora against the democratic Jewish state.*

—Professor Frederick Krantz
Director, Canadian Institute for Jewish Research
Professor (History), Liberal Arts College,
Concordia University, Montreal, Canada

This superb collection of incisive interviews of prominent academics and specialists on the demonization of Israel and the Jews by Manfred Gerstenfeld, is a volume which should be located on the bookshelves of every committed Jewish activist.

—Isi Leibler
Former Chairman Governing Board World Jewish Congress

Manfred Gerstenfeld's collection of interviews on anti-Semitism and its proxy, delegitimization of Israel, is brilliantly selected and encyclopedic in scope. His own essay tying the interviews together makes this required reading for those who want to understand where anti-Semitism is today.

—Richard B. Stone
Chairman Conference of Presidents of
Major American Jewish Organizations

GW00802490

Manfred Gerstenfeld

Demonizing Israel and the Jews

RVP Press

New York

SIMON
WIESENTHAL
CENTER
leadership with a global reach

RVP Publishers Inc.

95 Morton Street, Ground Floor

New York, NY 10014

RVP Press, New York

Photo cover: Associated Press / Manu Fernandez

The publication of this book was supported by the Simon Wiesenthal Center and International Center for Western Values, Amsterdam.

RVP Press™ is an imprint of RVP Publishers Inc., New York.
The RVP Publishers logo is a registered trademark of RVP Publishers Inc., New York.

Library of Congress Control Number: 2013935445

ISBN 978 1 61861 334 9

www.rvppress.com

In memory of Marianne

Table of Contents

God is punishing Israel for being a Socialist State

INTERVIEWS
DEMONIZING THE JEWS

Foreword

a genuine hatred not hate speech

I RECALL THE DAY in August 1977 when I met with Simon Wiesenthal, the fearless Nazi hunter, in his office in Vienna to ask him to bestow his good name on our new institution.

"It depends," he said. "If you are going to build an institution that only memorializes the past, then I will be happy to write you a letter of endorsement, but if you want my name, I am an activist, concerned about the future. I pursue Nazis as a warning to future generations, so that they will not make the same mistakes that we made by allowing hatred to go unanswered."

Thirty-five years later, Simon Wiesenthal would be appalled by the degree of anti-Semitism that has re-emerged in Europe, especially the growing parliamentary power of xenophobic and anti-Semitic parties in Greece, Hungary, and the Ukraine. He would be shocked that it has found so much traction in democracies—not only in Eastern Europe, but also in Western Europe and Scandinavia. He would be horrified by the apathetic response from those who, in a matter of seven decades, have forgotten their own past. Today, Holocaust denial and revisionism is a daily occurrence on the very continent that witnessed the mass murder of six million European Jews. Mr. Wiesenthal would be saddened, though not surprised, that the same rampant anti-Semitism has now infected the Arab world, its schools, media, and universities, and shows no sign of abating.

Its in the Koran from the beginning

I

As the founder of the Simon Wiesenthal Center, I have experienced it firsthand in meetings with top European leaders. When I raised the issue of anti-Semitism with then-French president Jacques Chirac during a meeting at the Elysee Palace in 2002, he said that there is no anti-Semitism in France. He then told us a story of a Palestinian student living in France whom he met on the campaign trail. When he shook the young man's hand and asked him what he was doing, the man said that he was studying at university. When Chirac asked him what he was going to do after he completed his studies, he said he would be going back to Palestine. "And what will you be doing there?" Chirac asked. "Killing Jews," he answered. "But why? Have they done anything to you?" "Yes, they have humiliated our people."

President Chirac was so shaken by the encounter that he invited the man to lunch at the Elysee Palace. Then the president told us he doubted whether he was able to change the young man's mind, but it just goes to show how frustrated Arabs are.

I remember then saying to President Chirac: "Mr. President, if there are any people who had reason to be humiliated, it was the survivors of the Holocaust who lost everything for no reason except that they were Jews. They were not murdered because they won a war, they were only murdered because they were born Jews. But what did they do about their feelings of humiliation? Did they blow up buses or planes? Did they strap themselves with suicide belts inside restaurants and nurseries? No, they learned how to redirect their lives, to pick themselves up by their bootstraps, rebuild their families and communities, and contribute greatly to humanity without hatred, seeking revenge, or blaming the world."

Immediately after we left the presidential palace, we went to a reception at the home of Baron De Rothschild. Two people from our group missed the bus and took a cab. They wore yarmulkes and were right outside the Baron's home when a few people started insulting them, saying things like "get out of France, you Jews."

It took many more ugly anti-Semitic incidents in France until President Chirac finally had to admit that there was anti-Semitism in his country. Today, the issue of whether Jews have a future in France remains an open question.

Until 2000, Muslim attacks against Jewish targets in Europe had mainly come from abroad. Since then, there have been several cases of murders by young Islamicized neighbors. These attacks must be seen in the context of the huge anti-Semitic incitement in large parts of the Muslim world. It targets Jews and Israelis without distinction.

Finally, anti-Semitism driven by hatred of the Jewish state too often goes unrecognized and unchallenged by European leaders, intellectuals, and the media. That is why this collection of essays is so important.

This book is the first one, to my knowledge, which illustrates with so many different examples how rampant contemporary hatred of Israel and the Jews is. Many aspects are illustrated in these short, but forceful interviews.

Demonizing Israel and the Jews is not easy reading, but it is a must for all those who are committed to combating and defeating those who seek to demonize and destroy our future.

One final note, world Jewry owes a deep debt of gratitude to our colleague, Dr. Manfred Gerstenfeld. Manfred is a noted and respected economist who combines a keen analytical mind with a passion to expose the truth and help us all understand the world's oldest hatred.

Rabbi Marvin Hier
Founder and Dean, Simon Wiesenthal Center

The Demonization of Israel and the Jews

— 1st error = "THE use of the word liberal is misleading": they are Socialists

EXTREME AND HATEFUL STEREOTYPES of the Jewish people have been around for over two thousand years. This has often led to disastrous consequences for Jews including mass murders, forced conversions, expropriation of possessions, and expulsions. The origin of anti-Semitism is commonly attributed to Egyptians. The first pogrom took place in Alexandria during Roman times.

For many centuries, the vilification of the Jews and Judaism was mainly executed by major forces in the Catholic Church. After Islam emerged and expanded in the seventh century, there was much defamation of Jews in Muslim societies. The sixteenth century Protestant reformer Martin Luther fervently demonized the Jews[1] as did many other church leaders. The current verbal attacks on Israel and calls for boycotts against it by various Protestant denominations, mainly liberal ones, draws new attention to Christian anti-Semitic positions. The same can be said for the World Council of Churches' attitude toward Israel. After the Holocaust, many believed that the mass genocide of the Jews would mean the end of socially acceptable anti-Semitism in the Western world. This was the more so, as Western societies gradually became aware of the multiple atrocities committed by Germans and Austrians in which they were aided by many other Europeans. This optimistic expectation has, however, not come true.

Latency and Mutation

Since the Second World War, important developments have taken place concerning anti-Semitism. Classic religious as well as ethnic/nationalistic anti-Semitism became latent, but did not disappear entirely in Europe. In this new century, it burst forth again with great intensity. One major manifestation of this can be seen in Hungary. The neo-fascist and anti-Semitic Jobbik Party received nearly 17 percent of votes in the 2010 parliamentary elections and became the country's third largest party. Anti-Semitism is a regular component of Hungarian public debate.

In Greece, the Golden Dawn Party, which has neo-Nazi leanings, has become more powerful in recent years. It entered parliament after both 2012 elections. By autumn 2012, the party received 14 percent of the votes in opinion polls.[2] Once such parties enter a country's parliament, they also gradually attain international positions. For instance, Golden Dawn member Eleni Zaroulia joined the Committee on Equality and Non-Discrimination of the Parliamentary Assembly of the Council of Europe in October 2012.[3]

In various countries, new radical parties have emerged. Some of them hold both positive and negative attitudes toward Jews and/or Israel. The Dutch anti-Islam PVV (Freedom Party), for instance, is very pro-Israel, yet strongly opposes ritual slaughter. While the party's main target on this issue is the Muslim population, the Dutch Jewish community suffers collateral damage from its stance.

Muslim Immigration

The massive Muslim immigration into Europe during the past decades has greatly increased anti-Semitism and anti-Israelism there. Segments from this community have caused an intensification of anti-Jewish and anti-

Israeli hate mongering in many European countries. Some Muslims have also committed extreme anti-Semitic crimes. In France, this was the case in the 2003 murder of Sébastien Selam, the kidnapping and subsequent murder of Ilan Halimi in 2006, and the 2012 murders of a teacher and three children in front of the Toulouse Jewish school Otzar HaTorah.[4]

A broad range of cases of anti-Semitism and anti-Israelism in Scandinavia show how these countries are falsely considered as model democratic societies. In 2009 during the Cast Lead campaign in Gaza, the largest anti-Semitic riots in Norway's history took place in Oslo. A Christian who walked to a pro-Israel demonstration with an Israeli flag was beaten and severely wounded. Projectiles which could have killed people were thrown at pro-Israel demonstrators. Almost all of the perpetrators were Muslims. Eirik Eiglad has described this in detail in a book titled *The Anti-Jewish Riots in Oslo*.[5]

Sweden's third largest city, Malmö, is often mentioned as the capital of European anti-Semitism. The perpetrators of many anti-Semitic acts there are mostly Muslims. Hannah Rosenthal, US Government special envoy for combating anti-Semitism, visited the town in 2012. She spoke out about anti-Semitic statements made by Social Democrat Mayor Ilmar Reepalu. Rosenthal also remarked that Malmö under this mayor is a "prime example" of "new anti-Semitism," as anti-Israel sentiment serves as a guise for Jew-hatred.[6] A record number of complaints about hate crimes in the city in 2010 and 2011 did not lead to any convictions.[7]

At the end of 2012, Arthur Avnon, Israeli ambassador to Denmark, was quoted as saying to the French press agency AFP, "We advise Israelis who come to Denmark and want to go to the synagogue to wait to don their skullcaps until they enter the building and not to wear them in the street, irrespective of whether the areas they are visiting are seen as being safe." He also advised visitors not to speak Hebrew loudly or wear visible Stars of David jewelry.[8] The main assaults against Jews are caused by Arabs. The Jewish community complains in vain about the inaction of the authorities.[9]

Anti-Semitism Mutates into Anti-Israelism

Another important postwar development is that anti-Semitism has broadened into a third major category, anti-Israelism. This form of anti-Semitism is characterized by similar hate motifs as religious and ethnic/nationalistic anti-Semitism. The common European working definition of anti-Semitism mentions a number of examples that define which attacks on Israel are anti-Semitic. These include the application of double standards to Israel by "requiring of it a behavior not expected or demanded of any other democratic nation."

Another anti-Semitic claim is that Jews are not entitled to self-determination, i.e., having a country of their own. A further example is the drawing of comparisons between contemporary Israeli policy and that of the Nazis.[10]

A 2011 study in seven countries by the University of Bielefeld on behalf of the German Friedrich Ebert Foundation illustrates that viewing Israel as having genocidal intentions toward the Palestinians—which is tantamount to Israel being a Nazi state—has profoundly permeated the mainstream of European societies. The study found that 63 percent of Poles think that Israel is conducting a war of extermination against the Palestinians. The lowest figures in the study concerned Italy and the Netherlands, where 38 percent and 39 percent of the population think so, respectively. In Hungary, Great Britain, Germany, and Portugal, between 40 percent and 50 percent hold these deeply anti-Semitic views.[11] The study illustrates that this criminal worldview with respect to Israel is widespread in mainstream Europe. That the study received little public attention is yet another indicator of the decaying norms and values of Europe.

The Simon Wiesenthal Center has published its ranking of those who disseminated the world's top ten anti-Semitic/anti-Israeli slurs in 2012. It lists Egypt's Muslim Brotherhood in first place, followed by the Iranian regime. Next in line are Brazilian cartoonist Carlos Latuff, Europe's anti-Semitic football fans, Ukraine's Svoboda Party, Golden Dawn in Greece, and Jobbik in Hungary. They are followed by the Norwegian Muslim convert Trond Ali Linstad, German journalist Jakob Augstein, and US Nation of Islam leader Louis Farrakhan.[12]

A Postmodern War

Israel is confronted with a major war by Arab states and their allies. This confrontation is postmodern in nature. Attackers do not always use all of the means at their disposal. This war is enduring, but not continuous, and manifests itself in many fragmented ways. One component is military and violent in nature. It expresses itself through wars, suicide attacks, and other terrorist assaults. Since Israel's withdrawal from Gaza in 2005, frequent rocket attacks and other terrorist activity from there are important elements of this kind of warfare.

Another facet of this huge confrontation with Israel is cyber war. Israel's Prime Minister Benjamin Netanyahu said in 2012 that many attempts are being made to infiltrate Israel's computerized systems, largely by Iranian cyber warfare. To combat this, Israel established a National Cyber Directorate in 2011.[13] Netanyahu also stated, "We are building a digital Iron Dome," indicating that Israel intends to make its system against cyber attacks as effective as the one against rocket strikes.[14]

A third category in this battle is the propaganda war. The following interviews indicate how multifaceted it is. One can easily add many other important subjects to the ones discussed in this book. Due to its fragmentation and the often indirect ways perpetrators phrase their anti-Semitism, the propaganda war is far more opaque than the other two.

How Anti-Semitism and Anti-Israelism Overlap

The three major forms of demonization of the Jews—religious anti-Semitism, nationalistic/ethnic anti-Semitism, and anti-Israelism—overlap.

Contemporary anti-Semites use a number of major hate motifs, which have been repeated in various forms over more than two thousand years. They all express one core motif: the Jews—nowadays also including Israel—embody "absolute evil." This motif recurs in many ways, parts of which are indirect rather than explicit.

The perception of "absolute evil" has changed over the centuries. In Christian anti-Semitism, the most evil act imaginable was that the Jews killed Jesus, whom many Christians believe to be God's son. Once societies turned more secular, God became less central.

In the newer ethnic/nationalist anti-Semitism, "absolute evil" was to have been born as an inferior human being. In Nazi belief, the Jews were considered "vermin and bacteria." This implied that Jews had to be exterminated. A contemporary hate variant claiming that Jews are inferior beings has its origins in the Koran, where Jews are called "sons of apes and pigs." Many Muslims take these Koran texts literally.

Nowadays, democracies accept the Universal Declaration of Human Rights which includes the statement that, "All human beings are born free and equal in dignity and rights."[15] However, many elsewhere disagree with part of this declaration. In 1990, the Organization of Islamic Countries accepted the Cairo Declaration of Human Rights in Islam.[16] Among its many human rights flaws is that it discriminates against religious minorities.[17]

In contemporary Western society, "absolute evil" is often seen as the crimes of the Germans and their allies during the Second World War, with the Holocaust as its paradigm. Extreme anti-Semites often call Israel a "Nazi state." Comparisons between Israelis and Nazis are commonplace in the Arab world. This "Holocaust inversion" is also often found in cartoons.[18] As mentioned before, many Europeans believe another version of this extreme defamation, namely that Israel intends to commit genocide against the Palestinians.

Submotifs are Identical

Not only the core motif of the three forms of anti-Semitism, but also their main submotifs are similar. One is: "Jews lust for power and money." Nowadays, this expresses itself as, "Jews control the United States" and "Jewish money controls the world."

A second submotif is that "Jews lust for blood and sex." Christian anti-Semites invented the blood libel. It claimed that "Jews needed the blood of a Christian child to make unleavened bread for Passover." A contemporary mutation of this libel is that Israel entered Gaza in 2008 in order to kill Palestinian women and children.

An organization financed by the Norwegian government paid for the trip of two Norwegian Hamas-supporting doctors to Gaza, during Israel's Cast Lead campaign in 2008–2009. These doctors promoted this contemporary blood libel in a book they wrote. On its back cover were comments made by former Conservative Norwegian Prime Minister Kare Willoch and then-Labor Party Foreign Minister of Norway, Jonas Gahr Støre.[19] This is only one among many examples of how Norwegian government ministers and members of the cultural elite support those who promote extreme anti-Israelism.

A third major anti-Semitic submotif is that Jews are "inhuman or inferior." In the anti-Israel version, this translates into, "Israel was born in sin and thus has no right to exist." These anti-Semites imply that all other nation states have the right to exist, even the most criminal ones such as Syria and Iran.

Verbal Demonization: Lies

[handwritten margin notes: "Not necessarily so depends if they profited in any case" and "Knowingly"]

To expose anti-Semitism and anti-Israelism, one has to understand how the demonization process of Israel functions. Its essence is the method of "a thousand cuts." There isn't one big attack on Jews and in particular on Israel, but many small ones. They are sometimes coordinated by perpetrators, yet also often not. For Israel's main Arab enemies, these attacks should lead to Israel's disappearance. Many of them say this explicitly. There are also non-Arab enemies of Israel who support them, for different reasons.

Verbal attacks play an important role in the propaganda war. One tool of verbal manipulation is lies. In religious anti-Semitism one of these is, "Jews killed the son of God." Leaving aside who Jesus was, this lie is extreme. Under Roman rule, Jews had no authority to kill anyone. Only the Roman rulers could decide to execute someone and the onus for Jesus' death was entirely upon them.

This lie was expanded even further by the claim that *all* Jews throughout generations should be held responsible for an act their forefathers had not committed. This is a profoundly immoral concept. In any situation, people should be held responsible for their own acts and not for those of their ancestors. During the Vatican 2 Council in 1965, the Catholic Church abandoned the position that the Jews committed deicide. However, some Christians continue to perpetuate this lie. The long history of the deicide charge illustrates how anti-Semitic lies are generated and how dangerous they can be for the Jews.

The blood libel is another major anti-Semitic lie. It originated in the English town of Norwich in the twelfth century. Its promoters invented this falsehood that Jews had killed a Christian child for ritual purposes. Since then and throughout the centuries, similar accusations have emerged mainly throughout Europe. This has often resulted in Christian persecutions of Jews.

New mutations of the blood libel are promoted nowadays, mainly as part of Arab propaganda. One example already mentioned is the lie that Israel entered Gaza in the 2008–2009 Cast Lead campaign with the main aim of killing Palestinian women and children. Another similar libel is that Israeli soldiers intentionally killed Palestinian child Muhammed al-Dura at the beginning of the second Intifada in 2000. According to an array of researchers, if the child was even killed at all, this was executed by the Palestinians. Israel has paid a very heavy price for not dealing adequately with Arab propaganda in this particular case.[20]

Another major lie is that the Jewish Temple, on the Temple mount where the Al Aksa mosque stands, never existed. This falsehood is part of a much broader structure of widespread lies which claim that the Jewish people have no linkage to the land of Israel.

The biggest contemporary anti-Semitic lie is Holocaust denial. This falsehood's underlying motive is to present the Jews as extreme villains. What the anti-Semites claim here is that Jews invented a huge mass murder of their own people by a third party, the Nazis and their allies, which, however, never took place. In this way, the lie continues: the Jews positioned themselves as major victims. Holocaust denial is widely spread in the Muslim world, yet also occurs elsewhere. In 2009, the major Norwegian TV2 television station broadcast an interview of more than a quarter of an hour with convicted British Holocaust denier David Irving.[21] The journalist who interviewed him displayed little knowledge of the topics discussed.

Verbal Demonization: Accusations and Exaggerations

Another tool of verbal demonization is through accusations about future activities for which there are no indications. One example is that Israel intends to destroy the Al Aksa Mosque.[22] Like the lies, these accusations are invented. One such false accusation, widely believed in Europe, has already been mentioned: "Israel intends to exterminate the Palestinians."

Another example of a widely spread false accusation about future actions to be undertaken by Israel was made by German Literature Nobel Prize winner Günther Grass. In a poem he wrote, he claimed—without providing any proof—that Israel intends to commit genocide on the Iranian people by launching atom bombs. This hate poem was published by major European dailies, the German *Süddeutsche Zeitung*,[23] the Italian *La Repubblica*, the British *The Guardian*, the Spanish *El Pais*, the Danish *Politiken*, and the Norwegian *Aftenposten*. Such widespread publication is so unusual for a poem, that this can only be explained by the anti-Israel attitudes of the papers' editors.

A third tool of verbal demonization is exaggeration. One major case of greatly overstating the number of Palestinian casualties by propagandists occurred after Israel's military operation in the Jenin refugee camp in 2002. This followed the murders by a Hamas suicide terrorist disguised as a woman in the Park Hotel in Netanya on Passover Eve. Thirty people were killed and 140 injured.[24]

During the battle in the Jenin refugee camp, about 55 Palestinians were killed—mainly armed fighters—as well as 23 Israeli soldiers. Several Palestinian leaders and spokesmen told the press thereafter that the number of Palestinians killed was ten or more times the actual figure. Spokesman Saeb Erekat also mentioned that the camp had been totally destroyed. Later it could be seen that the fighting had only affected a small part of the area.[25]

Fallacies

The use of lies, false accusations, and exaggerations as tools of demonization can be easily understood. Another type of hate propaganda is far more opaque—the use of fallacies. Three major categories of fallacies are emotional fallacies, ethical fallacies, and logical fallacies.[26] These groups in turn come in tens of sub-categories, including sentimental appeals, the application of faulty analogies, the use of double standards, the promotion of moral equivalence, the inversion of cause and result, conspiracy theories, bandwagon effects, and many more. They are complex manipulations of the truth, which require far more study.

The use of different standards concerning Jews when compared to others has been a major factor at the heart of anti-Semitic activity and incitement over many centuries. This was often easily understood, for instance, when Jews were confined to live in small areas of a town, were not free to dress in the clothes they wanted to wear, and could not work in most professions. This meant that double standards against them profoundly permeated most aspects of their lives. This discrimination of Jews was frequently accompanied by their demonization.

One category of double standards is biased reports or declarations. One clear example of this is the comparison of international reactions to the killing of Osama bin Laden by the US Army with those heard after Israel killed Hamas leader Sheikh Ahmed Yassin in 2004. Many politicians, who had condemned the targeted killing by the Israeli Defense Forces, praised the Americans for murdering bin Laden.

UN Secretary General Ban Ki-moon referred to the death of bin Laden as, "A watershed moment in our common global fight against terrorism." After the killing of Sheikh Yassin, then-UN Secretary General Kofi Annan said: "I do condemn the targeted assassination of Sheikh Yassin and the others who died with him. Such actions are not only contrary to international law, but they do not do anything to help the search for a peaceful solution."

During his tenure as British foreign secretary, Jack Straw called the killing of Sheikh Yassin "unacceptable" and "unjustified." The official

[handwritten note in top margin: "Cameron compared Gaza to a Concentration Camp...!!!"]

spokesman of then-Prime Minister Blair condemned the "unlawful attack" and observed: "We have repeatedly made clear our opposition to Israel's use of targeted killings and assassinations." British Prime Minister David Cameron congratulated President Obama on the success of the bin Laden assassination. Cameron considered it a massive step forward in the fight against extremist terrorism. Former Prime Minister Tony Blair also welcomed bin Laden's demise. Many more examples of these double standards can be given.[27]

The most frequent way double standards express themselves is through omissions. For instance, media may not or barely mention the rockets fired into Israeli population centers which eventually forced Israel to enter Gaza in the 2008–2009 Cast Lead military campaign. That same media may then place much emphasis on Israel's military actions.

Other forms of double standards include disproportional behavior. An example of this is when media report in detail on unfavorable news about Israel and barely mention extremely negative information about Muslim states. Other types are interference in Israel's internal affairs and different ways of applying international law concerning Israel and other countries.

Another important category of double standards might be called humanitarian racism. This is one of the least recognized forms of racism. It can be defined as attributing intrinsically reduced responsibility to people of certain ethnic or national groups regarding their criminal acts and intentions, even if they are major. Humanitarian racists judge misbehavior and crime differently according to the color and power of those who commit them. White people are held to different standards of responsibility than people of color are, for example.[28] Israelis are blamed for whatever measures they take to defend themselves. Palestinian responsibility for suicide bombings, murderous missile attacks, glorification of murderers of civilians, and promoting genocide is reduced, at best.

Part of the demonization process is carried out through the public call

[handwritten note in left margin: "Selective"]

for acts against Israel and/or the Jews. These acts can be violent or not. Inciting to terror is the most extreme form of verbal aggression. Others are calls for boycotts, divestment, or sanctions. Another one is condemnations, by the United Nations or the European Union, for instance. Yet another one is through distortion of international law. Any organization or individual intent on delegitimizing Israel can employ a cocktail of these methods. In order for this demonization to be successful, it needs to be repeated frequently. This is what Israel's Palestinian enemies and their Arab and Western allies have done for decades.

Transmitting Hate Themes

Those who demonize Israel and the Jews have a number of 'channels' to transmit their hate messages. Shouts of "Death to the Jews" have been heard during anti-Israel demonstrations in a variety of European cities. One can make hate statements on TV, or publish them in papers. Arab states and others can propose motions condemning Israel in the United Nations. One can create Israel-hate or anti-Semitic sites on the Internet and transmit demonizing statements in many ways through social media.

Another important method of transmitting hate messages is semantics. Language is not a neutral tool. If one uses the term "occupied territories," one employs language to bend international law, because they are actually "disputed territories."[29] Most Palestinian "refugees" did not flee from Israel. Their parents or grandparents may have done so and are genuine refugees. Another abuse of language is to call Israelis "colonists" if they live a few tens of kilometers from where they resided before. 'Peace' with Israel is seen by many Arabs as an intermediate stage for its destruction.

THE 'CRIMINAL' AL Qaeda Ideology — but
that is ISLAM &
the KORAN .!!

The Perpetrator Categories

Perpetrators of demonization come from many different backgrounds. Extreme anti-Semitic hate mongering is widespread in Arab and other Muslim countries. Major anti-Semitic incitement comes from many sources in the Muslim world, including government-controlled bodies of a country such as Egypt, which is officially at peace with Israel. For instance, in October 2012, a video showed Egyptian President Mohammed Morsi answering "Amen" to an imam who made a genocidal prayer request, "Oh Allah, destroy the Jews and their supporters."[30]

Currently the most extreme source of anti-Israel hatred and incitement is Iran. Its President Mahmoud Ahmadinejad and other leaders promote the destruction of Israel which can only be achieved through genocide. Yet this has not prevented Western government officials, religious leaders, and academics from hosting Ahmadinejad in their countries. Palestinian anti-Semitism also contains many genocidal elements. Hatred emitted from the Muslim world comes from far wider circles than the over 100 million supporters of the criminal Al Qaeda ideology, which aims for Jihad to bring about Muslim world rule.[31]

Segments of Muslim communities as well as Muslim preachers and leaders in the Western world are another major source of anti-Israelism and anti-Semitism. The nonselective mass immigration of Muslims into the Western world, and in particular into Europe, has been the most negative development for Jewish communities outside of Israel in the past fifty years. There are significant indications that the percentage of anti-Semites among Muslim immigrants is substantially higher than in the autochthonous populations. One aspect of this is that those who publicly shout "Death to the Jews" in street demonstrations seem to be largely Muslims.

Since Communism has crumbled in the former Soviet Union and its satellites, state-promoted or state-sponsored anti-Semitism has largely

MORE ALLOCHTHONOUS

disappeared there. It now mainly occurs in Arab and Muslim countries to varying degrees. However, in a number of other countries, anti-Israel positions of governments foster a societal climate conducive to anti-Semitism. The Chavez government in Venezuela is one such example.

Another perpetrator category comes from the extreme Right. It is enjoying a revival in Europe. In several Eastern European countries, this is partly stimulated by reactions to Communism and economic problems. In Western Europe, right-wing radicalization is fostered partly by problems related to mass immigration, poor government policies of integration of these immigrants, and anti-Western racism among some Muslim immigrant groups.

Politicians and others from the extreme Left and often those of Socialist parties also play a major role in the demonization of Israel. During Israel's Cast Lead campaign, for instance, leading Swedish Social Democrat politicians participated in anti-Israel demonstrations in which there were shouts of "Death to the Jews," swastikas, and banners of Arab terror movements which call for the destruction of Israel. In Norway, a government minister even participated in an anti-Israel demonstration.[32]

Media are another important perpetrator category. They often report about the Middle East in a one-sided, anti-Israel manner. They frequently ignore context and stress real or perceived negative acts committed by Israel, while regularly omitting crucial information about far more negative events in the Arab or Muslim world including Palestinian society.

One only has to measure newspaper space devoted to mass murders in the Syrian civil war and that devoted to Israel in mainly nonlethal actions against Palestinians to comprehend this media bias. According to the United Nations High Commissioner for Human Rights Navi Pillay, more than sixty thousand people were killed in Syria from March 2011 until the end of 2012.[33] In the Libyan civil war which lasted eight months from February 2011 until October 2011, an estimated thirty thousand people were killed according to the country's transitional government.[34]

DEMONIZING ISRAEL AND THE JEWS

Through editorial articles, the choice of op-eds, and decisions on whom to interview, media are originators of classic anti-Semitism and anti-Israelism. For many Muslim immigrants in Western countries, but sometimes also involving others, there is no distinction between Jews and Israel. Biased media information thus indirectly leads to physical and verbal attacks on local Jews as well.

With the increased importance of the Internet, there are many anti-Semites and demonizers of Israel among those who use it for this purpose. Many of them come out of the Muslim world, the extreme Right, and the extreme Left.

Anti-Israel and anti-Semitic activities in academia manifest themselves through biased teaching, boycott proposals, divestment initiatives, discrimination against Jews identifying with Israel, and sometimes classic anti-Semitic acts. On a number of campuses in certain countries, such initiatives recur. The main ones are Great Britain, Canada, and the United States. Anti-Israel teachers are often clustered worldwide within certain disciplines, such as Middle Eastern studies and linguistics.[35]

Non-governmental organizations (NGOs) are in the forefront of attacks on Israel. Many of these have an anti-Semitic character. Ongoing documentation on humanitarian NGOs as anti-Israel hate mongers, is provided by the research organization NGO Monitor.[36]

Several Christian organizations in the United States, Canada, Europe, and developing countries play an important role in anti-Israel activities. One finds active Christian anti-Israel currents in various mainstream Protestant denominations. They often propose discriminatory measures against Israel, without suggesting taking any action against other countries which are extreme human rights abusers. Theological factors sometimes play a major role in Christian anti-Semitic activities. While some of the acts of anti-Semitism originators in various fields such as some media, academia, NGO, and the United Nations are regularly monitored by various bodies,

NGO is a Misdirection they are all pretty much without exception taxpayer funded in one way or another ?? ARE GOVERNMENT

this is not the case for Christian anti-Semitism.

In some countries, trade unions are at the forefront of the anti-Israel battle. They promote discriminatory actions against Israel while abstaining from activism against notorious human rights offenders in many countries. This happens for instance in Great Britain, Ireland,[37] Belgium, Norway, Canada, and South Africa.

The United Nations becomes an abetter of anti-Semitism whenever its organizations and staff members discriminate against Israel.[38, 39, 40] A significant number of scholars and professionals in the international law field play an important role in promoting selective accusations against Israel regarding human rights and other laws.

Teaching prejudice about Israel and Jews in schools has two important sources: biased textbooks and biased teachers. Regarding the former, studies are available in some countries. Only anecdotal information is available about the latter.[41]

Anti-Israelism is also promoted by some Israelis and Jews. It is often poorly understood that Jews, Israeli or not, can be anti-Semites just like anyone else. Anti-Semitism is defined according to certain statements or attitudes. If Jews or Israelis hold such opinions, they are therefore anti-Semites. Some of these people believe that by participating in the delegitimization of Israel, this will make them acceptable in their political environment. Others are influenced by anti-Israel media and members of societal elites.

When discussing demonization, one also needs to analyze what impact delegitimization has already made on Diaspora Jews and on Israel. This concerns issues such as the need for major security measures, Jews hiding their identity, and many others.

What — such as Christian Socialists which is oxymoronic

Exposing Anti-Israelism

The increasing delegitimization of Israel is already quite powerful and far-reaching. A large number of the interviews included in this book expose many aspects of this. The first step which should be taken in order to be able to fight the demonization of Israel and the Jews in a more effective way, is to understand how enemies operate. This book exposes their actions in a number of areas.

The battle against the demonization of Jews and Israel requires a much more dedicated effort. At present, the Israeli and Jewish sides provide a fragmented and inefficient picture. Initially, the fight against demonization will need a much better organizational structure. Researchers will have to analyze and understand the delegitimization war in great detail and follow its developments systematically.

Thereafter, they will have to develop a strategy for the various battle-fields. Their task will also be to mobilize others and interact with those who are already fighting delegitimization. In this way, techniques will develop and improve over the course of time. It will also require a change in the mentality and mode of thinking of the defenders of Israel and the Jews. One aspect of this is that offense is frequently better than defense.

Enemies of Israel and the Jews will have to be convinced that if they attack, there will be a heavy price to pay. Exposing the double standards, the duplicity, the lies, false accusations, exaggerations, and fallacies of the attackers may not only hinder their actions, but in the long run, will most likely hurt them as well.

Is this a Socialist trying to fix Socialism.

Until Socialism is called out — Anti Semitism won't go anytime soon

INTERVIEWS
DEMONIZING ISRAEL

Israel, the European Commission, Europe, and the Netherlands

F ROM 1999–2004, FRITS BOLKESTEIN was the European Union's commissioner responsible for the internal market, taxation, and customs union. Before that, he had been the Dutch defense minister and leader of the Liberal Party, VVD. In 2005, he became a professor—on the subject of intellectual background to political developments—at both Leiden University and the Technical University of Delft.

Bolkestein observed: "The Israeli 'file' in the European Commission is a difficult one because so many factors come into play. Israel has undoubtedly lost a publicity battle. This, however, is only one factor that plays a role. Another is that people defer to numbers. There are hundreds of millions of Arabs and less than eight million Israelis. Third, there is the oil issue. Oil contracts are negotiated on a bilateral basis and this makes them highly political. The Arabs have an abundance of oil and could someday impose an embargo once again. The Netherlands already had that experience in 1973.

"A fourth factor is the influence of so many European Muslims with their electoral power on foreign policy. I met Dominique de Villepin, when he was the foreign minister of France, at a Bilderberg conference and asked him how French foreign policy had been affected by the presence of five to six million Muslims. He replied: 'Not at all.' This was not very convincing.

"A fifth factor that further complicates the issue is a guilt complex toward Jews and Israel. This applies first and foremost to Germany. But it is important in the Netherlands too, mainly because about 75 percent of Dutch Jews were murdered in the Holocaust. Nowadays that feeling has rather faded, and I do not think it is still significant in other European countries.

"Sixth is the anti-Semitism, which in Europe can also influence the political sphere. It often dresses up as anti-Israelism. David Pryce-Jones once discussed in detail in a *Commentary* article, the barely concealed anti-Semitism in the French Foreign Service.

"I am not enough of an expert to assess whether that is true. I do however recall de Gaulle calling the Jews 'a domineering and arrogant people' in 1967. One doesn't make such remarks innocently. If the French say, somewhat heatedly, 'we aren't anti-Semitic, and certainly not our foreign service,' I question that. I remember well the daily *Le Monde's* cartoon on that occasion, showing a Jew in concentration camp clothing, standing in a provocative pose like Napoleon, with one foot on barbed wire."

Bolkestein spoke at the remembrance ceremony in Amsterdam for the sixty-fifth anniversary of Kristallnacht in November 2003, where he said: "The heart of the Middle East conflict is Arab unwillingness to accept Israel's existence. Muslim terrorism against Europe is not the result of the Israeli-Palestinian conflict. It is directed against Western culture, which many Muslims see as a threat."

According to Bolkestein, all the aforementioned issues have to be viewed in the context of Europe's present problems. One subject that preoccupies him is what he calls European "self-hatred." In the inaugural lecture for his professorship he said: "An important question is why and when Western Europeans, in general and the Dutch in particular, lost their self-confidence. In my view this goes back to the First World War, the confusion of the interbellum, the Second World War, and the murder of the Jews. All this has been reinforced by the cultural revolution of 1968 and the years thereafter."

He adds: "Judging by the standards of the Universal Declaration of Human Rights, the dominant civilization of Europe at present is superior to Islamic civilization. All civilization is based on judgments. I believe that the civilization of Rome was superior to that of Gaul. I also consider Unionist America superior to the slaveholder Confederacy, and democratic postwar West Germany superior to Communist East Germany."

Bolkestein remarks: "In the European Commission, I twice tried to raise the problem of the multicultural society and the risks of unlimited Muslim immigration. My colleagues were ten years behind the Netherlands on this issue and did not want to discuss it. I said to one commissioner that they almost considered me a racist. He replied: 'Drop the word almost.'"

In 2010, Bolkestein said: "Jews have to realize that there is no future for them in the Netherlands and that they best advise their children to leave for the United States or Israel." He arrived at this conclusion due to problems he foresaw in the Netherlands, specifically resulting from the unsuccessful integration of many Muslim immigrants and the difficulties this would create for conscious Jews. This caused a major public debate. Simultaneously many articles were published describing the current harassment of recognizable Jews in the Netherlands.

Language as a Tool
against Jews and Israel

GEORGES-ELIA SARFATI, **professor of linguistics at the Sorbonne in Paris, has researched the relationship between opinion and discourse. He demonstrates how loaded language can be by examining the expression "anti-Zionism" as an example. In his book** *The Captive Nation*, **he devotes many pages to how anti-Zionism emerged in the Soviet Union.**

"Most people think that language, and in particular speech, is transparent and that it serves to transmit information. All words have a history, which have an impact on their use, even if people are not aware of this. Rather than words being neutral, they serve to introduce a certain vision of the question one addresses.

"This is particularly clear in the case of anti-Semitism and its manifestations, including anti-Zionism. When analyzing the various phenomena of Judeophobia, one discovers an archive of words used against the Jews over the centuries. It aims to criminalize all forms of Jewish identity: spiritually as religious anti-Judaism; culturally as anti-Semitism, and socio-politically as anti-Zionism."

Sarfati explains: "It was the Soviet Union's Ministry of Information which began to use the expression 'anti-Zionism' systematically after the Six-Day War. From the Soviet press, it migrated to the media of the French extreme

Left. Prior to that, the word's use was sporadic at most. It did not appear in dictionaries until the 1970s. One has to recall however, that Hitler claimed in *Mein Kampf* that Zionism was the bridgehead of the 'Jewish conspiracy.' Anti-Zionism's major 'canonic' texts are first and foremost Soviet fabrications. One of the supreme Soviet ideologists, Trofim Kitchko, published several anti-Semitic books between 1963 and the beginning of the 1980s. His first one, *Judaism Unembellished*, was sponsored by the Academy of Sciences.

"Marxism had negated the idea of Jewish sovereignty; Stalinism radicalized this view. Propaganda techniques of the Nazis were recycled by the Soviets. When parts of the Arab world were influenced by the Soviet Union, their propaganda apparatus appropriated itself of the anti-Zionist discourse.

"Third Worldism has also appropriated itself of the anti-Zionist discourse. This movement is characterized by an ideological and political commitment toward the world's poorer countries and also supports revolutionary action. Third Worldism has developed its own linguistic arms, deriving from Marxist ideology.

"They enabled Marxists to resuscitate claims no longer fashionable and to find a new echo for them in Europe, where they are promoted by so-called progressives, i.e., Maoists and Trotskyites. In another linguistic construction, Palestinian claims against Israel were redefined in the terminology of Third Worldism.

"From the point of view of language, anti-Zionism thus becomes a tool to federate and create coalitions of extremely diverging opinions. This sociological phenomenon, which developed over half a century, has by now become an 'ideology'—a system of ideas—which has permeated various specific groups in society."

Sarfati develops this concept in detail in his book *Anti-Zionism*. He says: "A number of key equations dominate the anti-Zionist discourse. The master one—which transversally commands all others—is 'Zionism equals Nazism.' The various types of anti-Israel propaganda have been circulated and repeated endlessly. It could only permeate society because of the latter's anti-Semitic infrastructure. It then further developed into other falsifications such as 'Israel uses "the final solution" in the Middle East toward the Palestinians, which was applied against the Jews in Europe.'

"A second equation was derived from the first: 'Israel equals racism.' This is based on historical notions about racism. One only has to replace the word 'blacks' with 'Palestinians' in the statement: 'Blacks are second class citizens in their own country.' Other variants are 'Israel practices segregation,' 'Israel conducts an apartheid policy,' or 'The territories are Bantustans.'

"The American linguist Noam Chomsky—a Jewish Israel-defamer—has played a major role in the development of this terminology. He wishes to dissolve Israel into a binational state. His anti-Zionism is part and parcel of his anti-Americanism. For half a century, he has maintained that Israel is an instrument of American politics. His pseudoradical theories are based on the 'victimology' concept, claiming that non-Westerners are eternal victims of imperialism.

"A third equation, which is also derived from the first one, is 'Zionism is colonialism.' It is accompanied by a fourth one: 'Zionism is imperialism.' Thereafter, these equations can be synthesized into one: The 'Zionist, fascist, racist, and colonial state.'"

Sarfati says that one has to realize the strategic effectiveness of this attack. "These equivalencies are so evil because they attach the four major negative characteristics of Western history in the last century—Nazism, racism, colonialism, and imperialism—to the State of Israel.

"The anti-Zionist propaganda conveys that you only have to be, for instance, against Nazism—and who is not?—to be an anti-Zionist. The language of these pseudoequations and pseudoequivalences supports every initiative hostile to Zionism and turns it into an act of progressiveness and humanism. Many people who support this do not realize that they join the millennia-old list of anti-Semites."

Major Anti-Israeli and Anti-Semitic
Motifs in Arab Cartoons

JOËL KOTEK, a political scientist, is professor at the Free University of Brussels. He has collected many thousands of anti-Semitic cartoons, mainly from Arab media. These cartoons not only target Israel, but aim at all Jews. His research resulted in a book titled Cartoons and Extremism: Israel and the Jews in Arab and Western media.

Kotek stresses that in a world where image plays a central role, the cartoon has become a popular and efficient means of communication. A caricature may have as much influence on public opinion as an editorial.

"The collective image of the Jews created by Arab cartoons lays the groundwork for a possibility of genocide. One can argue about whether these genocidal ideas are conscious or subconscious."

Kotek adds: "The main recurrent theme in these cartoons is 'the devilish Jew.' By extension, this image suggests that the Jewish religion must be diabolic, and the entire Jewish people evil. These cartoons convey the idea that Jews behave like Nazis, leading readers to conclude that the only logical solution is their elimination. As the Arab world has become increasingly convinced of these ideas, they have no inhibitions showing them on a multitude of websites."

Several hundred Arab cartoons from Kotek's collection are categorized according to anti-Semitic themes in his book: "The first theme is based on the oldest anti-Semitic motif, demonization of the Jew. The Jew is depicted as inhuman and an enemy of humanity. This dehumanization is necessary to justify the hoped for elimination.

"On 28 December 1999—well before the second Palestinian uprising—*Al-Hayat al-Jadida*, the official Palestinian Authority journal, published a cartoon expressing this core idea. It depicted an old man in a djellaba, symbolizing the twentieth century, taking leave of a young man wearing a tee-shirt symbolizing the twenty-first century. In between them stood a small Jew with a Star of David on his breast, above which an arrow pointed to him saying, 'the illness of the century.'

"A second central theme in anti-Semitic cartoons is the Jew as a murderer of God. This is originally a Christian motif. This representation by Muslims serves in efforts to obtain the sympathy of some Christians by adapting one of their central myths.

"Another major motif is Israel as a Nazi state. This is based on two contradictory allegations, which the Islamists try to reconcile. Their first claim is that the Shoah never happened. Their second contention is that if it did, it has caused more damage to the Palestinians because they believe they are being treated worse than the Nazis treated the Jews."

Kotek remarks: "The next motif—zoomorphism—is a very common theme throughout the world. To abuse one's adversaries, one dehumanizes them by turning them into animals. In Nazi, Soviet, and Romanian caricatures, the Jew is often depicted as a spider, perceived as an evil animal. The two other predominant anti-Semitic zoomorphic motifs are the bloodthirsty vampire and the octopus. The vampire image is a classic theme used by anti-Semites. I have not found any other people besides the Jews represented as such. This genocide-preparing design originates in Christian imagination. The Arab cartoonists often follow the Nazis as far as the bestial representation of the Jews is concerned. The messages transmitted are that the Jews are destructive, inhuman, and evil.

"The fifth anti-Semitic motif in Arab cartoons echoes the classic conspiracy theme, that 'the Jews control the world.' Israel's opponents allege that the Jews dominate the United States. By implication, they also claim that the Jews are the 'masters of the world'—a classic conspiracy theme exploited by the Nazis.

"Yet another major theme in Arab cartoons is the blood-loving or blood-thirsty Jew. This motif also originates in Christian anti-Semitism. In today's Arab world, this image of unbridled hatred has mutated into the alleged quest for Palestinian blood. There are so many of these cartoons that I could select only a few for my book. Blood-drinking Jews are frequently shown by *Al Ahram*, one of Egypt's leading dailies. On 21 April 2001, it printed a cartoon showing an Arab being put into a flatting mill by two soldiers wearing helmets with Stars of David. The Arab's blood pours out and two Jews with *kippot* and Stars of David on their shirts drink the blood laughingly.

"Another recurring anti-Semitic theme in Arab cartoons is the most extreme. The concept that the Jews not only murder, but preferably target children, is what the cartoonists try to convey through their imagery. This depicts the Palestinians primarily as children or babies."

Kotek concludes that these caricatures often express a new type of anti-Semitism. "They are frequently 'calls for murder.' To the cartoonists, death seems the only worthy punishment that 'the Zionist enemy' merits."

The UN "Zionism Is Racism" Resolution Revisited

Y OHANAN MANOR is the chairman of IMPACT-SE, which surveys school curricula and textbooks to check their conformity with international standards. He is a former lecturer at the Hebrew University and was director general of the Information Department of the World Zionist Organization. His book *To Right a Wrong* (1996) analyzes the revocation of the "Zionism is Racism" resolution.

"More than twenty years ago, the infamous 'Zionism is Racism' resolution was repealed. We have seen many new efforts since then to delegitimize Israel. The Israeli government and opinion leaders need to understand what happens if Israel does not develop appropriate strategies against delegitimization actions in the international arena. Therefore, it is instructive to analyze summarily how this UN resolution came into being in 1975, what happened thereafter, and how it was finally overturned."

Manor says: "The idea of having Zionism condemned by the United Nations originated with the Soviet Union in the mid-1960s, before the Six-Day War. It stemmed from the Soviet refusal to have anti-Semitism condemned by the UN. This occurred in 1964 and 1965 during the negotiation of the International Convention on the Elimination of All Forms of Racial Discrimination within the framework of the UN Commission on Human Rights. Since the Soviet Union could not openly voice such a position, it conditioned its acceptance of condemning anti-Semitism on a demand to denounce Zionism and Nazism.

"Subsequently, the Six-Day War in 1967 inflicted a severe blow on the Soviet Union's weaponry and prestige. It then developed a more militant policy to regain and enlarge its influence in the Middle East. It was based on a near-total backing of the Palestinian Liberation Organization. Initially, this approach went well. Then came major setbacks, including the expulsion of Soviet advisers from Egypt, the Israeli-Egyptian disengagement negotiations of November 1973, and the Israeli-Syrian disengagement agreement of May 1974 with the active involvement of the United States. This apparently led to a Soviet-PLO plan to bring about Israel's expulsion from the United Nations, with the PLO taking its place.

"On 22 November 1974, the PLO obtained UN Observer status as a national liberation movement. In August 1975, the Organization of African Unity explicitly referred to depriving Israel of 'its status as member.' At the UN General Assembly on 1 October 1975, Ugandan dictator Idi Amin called 'for the expulsion of Israel from the United Nations and the extinction of Israel as a state.'

"In July 1975, the Soviet Union and the PLO succeeded in having Zionism explicitly condemned at the UN International Women's Year conference in Mexico City, which stressed in its final declaration that 'Peace requires the elimination of colonialism, neocolonialism, foreign occupation, Zionism, apartheid, and racial discrimination in all its forms.' In August 1975, the Organization of African Unity in Kampala stated that 'the racist regime in occupied Palestine and the racist regime in Zimbabwe and South Africa have a common imperialist origin . . . organically linked in their policy aimed at repression of the dignity and integrity of the human being'; while the Non-Aligned conference in Lima 'severely condemned Zionism as a threat to world peace.'

"Western and above all American opposition to Israel's expulsion or suspension, notably an American warning that such a move would force the United States to reassess its UN membership, thwarted the initiative. However, it increased the eagerness to advance as a substitute the condemnation of Zionism as racism. This was formally achieved first within the framework of the Third Committee of the General Assembly on 16 October 1975, and then on 10 November 1975 by the UN General Assembly plenary with Resolution 3379 (XXX), which 'Determines that Zionism is a form of racism and racial discrimination.' The Soviet-Arab coalition won by 72–35 with two abstentions.

"During 1976–1984, the 'Zionism is Racism' resolution was reiterated time and again, sometimes by even larger majorities. Even more far-reaching motions were adopted in other UN bodies. Zionism began to assume 'mythical proportions in international discourse as a global cause of most world problems.' This trend also substantially penetrated Western circles, especially universities.

"The Israeli and Jewish world viewed the resolution with disdain. For a long time there were no Israeli attempts to act for the resolution's revocation. This nonsensical position was maintained for almost a decade. Only then it was acknowledged by official Israel that the resolution needed to be fought directly and not as another expression of anti-Semitism. From the time Israel woke up, it would take more than five years to overturn 'Zionism is Racism.'

"This repeal was finally achieved not only thanks to the end of the Cold War, but first and foremost because the United States took the lead and invested massively in the revocation endeavor, in spite of manifest reluctance and feet dragging by the State Department, which was substantially overcome due to Senator Daniel Moynihan banging on the table. President George H.W. Bush gave 'unprecedented instructions to all his ambassadors [to warn] countries that failure to vote for revoking the resolution could affect their ties with the United States.' Finally, the draft resolution for repeal was sponsored by eighty-six states and passed by 111–25 with thirteen abstentions on December 16, 1991."

Terrorism Targeting Jewish Communities and Israelis Abroad

MICHAEL WHINE **is director of government and international affairs at the Community Security Trust, the defense organization of British Jewry. He has published extensively on terrorism and other subjects.**

"In March 2012, Mohammed Merah murdered a Jewish teacher and three children in front of a Jewish school in Toulouse, France. In July 2012, five Israeli tourists and a Bulgarian were killed by a suicide bomber at Burgas Airport, Bulgaria. These attacks, and others planned but intercepted, have once again focused attention on terrorism against Diaspora Jewish communities and Israeli targets abroad.

"This terrorism is the most violent manifestation of contemporary anti-Semitism. It is proof that the lives of any Jew or Israeli abroad are threatened. The damaging impact that a successful mass-casualty terrorist attack would have on Jewish communal life is huge. That is why Jewish communities in Europe invest far more effort and money on security at their communal buildings than similar organizations."

Whine: "Many terrorist groups are profoundly anti-Semitic. It is a common conviction across different extremist ideologies that Jews, Zionism, or Israel are preventing the creation of a new, better world. Yet Jews are currently not the prime target for many terrorists; the United States and other countries with military forces in Afghanistan are. The extent to which terrorists consider Jews a primary target may depend in part on what role traditional anti-Semitic stereotypes play in their worldview.

"Among the sources of terrorism against Jews and Israelis outside Israel, the Salafi jihadist variety is the most dangerous. There are many indications that it is on the rise. Before that, the main perpetrators of anti-Jewish terrorism had been Palestinian secular terrorists. Others were violent extremists from diverse backgrounds, e.g., neo-Nazis, Marxist-Leninists, anarchists, Arab nationalists, Khomeinite revolutionaries, and radical Sunni Islamists. Of the fifty-one recorded attacks and intercepted plots from 2002 to 2010, thirty-nine were carried out by Al-Qaeda, its affiliates, Lashkar-e-Toiba, and others motivated by the global jihad movement. Historically, links between different terrorist movements have existed, though it is more accurate to view each as independent.

"The most lethal terrorist act was the truck bomb attack on the Buenos Aires Asociación Mutual Israelita Argentina (AMIA) headquarters in July 1994. Eighty-five people were killed. We know since then that it was ordered by Iranian government leaders. During the 1980s and 1990s, Iran and Hezbollah repeatedly carried out terrorist attacks on Jewish or Israeli targets outside Israel. They included the bombings of Jewish communal institutions in Paris in September 1986 by Lebanese Shiites under Hezbollah control; a failed car bombing against a Jewish community building in Bucharest in 1992, later discovered to have been carried out by Hezbollah; and the failed ambush of Turkish Jewish leader Jak V. Kamhi in 1993 by an Iran-linked group.

"Ayman al-Zawahiri, now the leader of Al-Qaeda, issued several calls to attack Jews in addition to Israelis. In his 2001 book *Knights under the Prophet's Banner* he wrote: 'Tracking down the Americans and the Jews is not impossible. Killing them with a single bullet, a stab, or a device made up of a popular mix of explosives or hitting them with an iron rod is not impossible. Burning down their property with Molotov cocktails is not difficult. With the available means, small groups could prove to be a frightening horror for the Americans and the Jews.'

"In 2008, al-Zawahiri endorsed 'every operation against Jewish interests' and promised to 'strive as much as we can to deal blows to the Jews inside Israel and outside it.' Shortly thereafter, he released a videotape in which he responded to a question as to why Al-Qaeda avoided attacking Israel: 'Does the person asking the question not know that Al-Qaeda struck the Jews in Djerba, Tunisia, and Israeli tourists in their hotel in Mombasa? We promise our Muslim brothers that we will do our best to strike the Jews both inside and outside Israel, and with the help of Allah, we will succeed.'

"There are many other radical Muslim religious leaders who call for murder. For example, supreme guide of the Muslim Brotherhood in Jordan, Sheikh Himam Sa'id, stated in an address to Palestinians in Hebron that 'you are now waging a war against the Jews. You are well versed in this. We saw how, on a day in 1929, you slaughtered the Jews in Hebron. Today, slaughter them in the land of Hebron. Kill them in Palestine.'

"British, American, Israeli, and other security services have sometimes publicized their interception of terrorist plots against Jewish and Israeli targets. Jewish communities continue to receive discreet alerts to enhance security at communal buildings. However, their security situation is unlikely to improve in the coming years, although there is now a greater recognition of the threats they face."

Taking Iran and Hamas Leaders
Before an International Court?

RETIRED AMBASSADOR ALAN BAKER **is one of Israel's leading international law experts. He served as legal counsel and deputy director general of Israel's Ministry for Foreign Affairs between 1996 and 2004, followed by four years (2004–2008) as Israel's ambassador to Canada. He is presently the director of the Institute for Contemporary Affairs at the Jerusalem Center for Public Affairs.**

"International courts and tribunals could provide a number of opportunities for Israel to act against those seeking its destruction. To prevent future genocide, which is the greatest crime in the world, the Convention on the Prevention and Punishment of the Crime of Genocide, 1948—better known as the UN Genocide Convention—was adopted. According to its Articles 3 and 9, complaints against a state responsible for genocide, for conspiracy to commit it, for direct and public incitement to commit it, for attempted genocide, and for complicity in genocide, may be referred to the International Court."

Baker: "Iran and its leaders have been openly and systematically inciting genocide against Israel for over a decade. Since 1956, Iran has been a party to the UN Genocide Convention and may thus be brought before the International Court of Justice in The Hague (ICJ) for violating the

[handwritten marginalia: Just plain Murder is the greatest Crime]

42

convention. Additionally, since Article 4 of the Genocide Convention removes any claim of immunity or exemption for a head of state or government, Iran's President Mahmoud Ahmadinejad and Supreme Leader Ali Khamenei can be prosecuted before the International Criminal Court (ICC) pursuant to the 1998 Rome Statute of the International Criminal Court (ICC). However, since Iran has not yet become a party to this statute, any complaint against Iranian leaders would have to be referred to the ICC by the UN Security Council or initiated by the court's prosecutor." Baker remarks: "Article 25 of the ICC Statute mentions various degrees of involvement in one or more of the crimes listed, whether this be incitement to genocide or crimes against humanity, or aiding and abetting, soliciting, attempting, or otherwise, regarding such crimes.

"While, as a general rule, all international conventions are voluntarily entered into by states at their sovereign discretion, there are certain circumstances in which a state may be obliged to fulfill its obligations, pursuant to a convention to which it is party, or to be punished for such violation. Thus, if the UN Security Council decides to refer to the ICC a complaint against the leaders of Iran for incitement to genocide, this would be obligatory.

"A major problem in the case of Iran is that international law and practice are, to a very large extent, driven by political will. Hence, when President Ahmadinejad was in the United States for meetings in the UN and he was invited to make a presentation at Columbia University, no one acted to seek his arrest. This despite the fact that it could have been done theoretically, had the United States or any other state petitioned the Security Council."

Baker adds: "Hamas is also an example of blatant incitement to genocide, pursuant to the terms of its charter. Yet the leaders of Hamas, Hezbollah, Fatah, and other terror groups and organizations cannot be brought before the International Court of Justice because the court, pursuant to its statute, only deals with states. They therefore do not come within the court's jurisdiction. Individual members of Hamas and other terror organizations could be brought before the ICC if a country that chooses to arrest them accepts the jurisdiction of the court and fails to place these people on trial before its own tribunals. Similar to the Ahmadinejad situation, the Security Council could theoretically be asked to institute a prosecution against a representative of Hamas or other terror organizations.

"In order to subpoena these Hamas members, one could not use the crime of terrorism, as it is not yet listed as a crime in the ICC Statute. There are, however, several crimes listed under 'Crimes against Humanity' such as murder, imprisonment, or severe deprivation of liberty and attacks directed against civilian population. Others concern 'War Crimes' such as willful killing, injuring, or causing great suffering; hostage taking; attacking civilian populations, civilian objects such as towns and villages, religious and cultural buildings; as well as attempts at genocide. These could be attributed to representatives of Hamas or any of the other terror groups.

"One should further note that those who support, sponsor, finance, and encourage Hamas and other terror organizations can also be accused theoretically under the Genocide Convention of 'conspiracy to commit genocide,' 'direct and public incitement to commit genocide,' and 'complicity or attempted genocide.'

"In the meantime, the Palestinian Authority is seeking to utilize international courts in order to harm Israel. This is a development that will gain momentum, as in November 2012, the UN upgraded Palestinian status to a non-member state. That could give them the legal capacity to chase Israel in international courts and tribunals.

"To sum up, we can assume that there will be future attempts to use these legal means in conflicts in the Middle East. Therefore, Israel should analyze what it can legally do against those seeking to harm it or its leadership on the one hand and prevent these legal options from being used against it on the other hand."

Existing Tools to Deal with Iran's Crimes

IRWIN COTLER **is a member of the Canadian Parliament for the Liberal Party, emeritus professor of law at McGill University, and former minister of justice and attorney general of Canada. He is cochair of the Inter-Parliamentary Group for Human Rights in Iran.**

"Ahmadinejhad's Iran—I use that term to distinguish it from the people and publics of Iran who are targets of massive domestic repression—constitutes a clear and present danger to international peace and security, to regional and Middle East stability, and increasingly, and alarmingly so, to its own people.

"We are witnessing in Ahmadinejhad's Iran the toxic convergence of four distinct yet interrelated threats: nuclear, genocidal incitement, terrorism, and massive violations of human rights."

Cotler says: "Iran is in standing violation of international legal prohibitions with respect to its nuclear weaponization program. Iran supports Syria's Bashar al-Assad killing his own people. It is also the world's leading state sponsor of terrorism, killing innocents from Argentina to Lebanon, Afghanistan to Syria. Furthermore, it has the highest per capita rate of executions of minors worldwide.

"In particular, Iran's state-sanctioned incitement to hate and genocide has been persistent, pervasive, and pernicious, yet little attention has been paid to the imperative of legal remedy. A website affiliated with Iranian Supreme Leader Ali Khamenei declared in February 2012 that Iran would be justified in killing all Israeli Jews. This Tehran's long-range missiles could accomplish in nine minutes, boasted the site. Khamenei, for his part, called Israel a 'cancerous tumor that must be removed.' He has also declared that there is 'justification to kill all the Jews and annihilate Israel, and Iran must take the helm.' As an all-party report of the Canadian Parliament concluded, Iran has already committed the crime of incitement to genocide prohibited under international law.

"Yet a panoply of remedies exist to combat it. State parties to the UN Genocide Convention should file complaints against Iran—which is also party to the convention—before the International Court of Justice. Member states should request that the UN Security Council pass a resolution condemning Iran's incitement to genocide and refer the matter to the International Criminal Court, which can indict Khamenei, Ahmadinejad, and their collaborators, as it has Sudanese President Omar al-Bashir. This threat of criminal prosecution should be added to existing diplomatic and economic pressures meant to deter terrorism and nuclear-weapon development by Tehran.

"In counteracting the Iranian wave of state terror, the international community should hold the perpetrators to account. Otherwise, a culture of impunity continues to encourage terrorism itself. All states have the responsibility to use all instruments at their disposal to confront Iranian terrorist aggression. These include, for instance, increasing bilateral and multilateral diplomatic and economic sanctions, the mobilization of political pressure to isolate the Iranian regime as a pariah among the nations, the naming and shaming of Iranian perpetrators and their Hezbollah proxies to combat Iranian denial of their culpability, and bringing these perpetrators to justice.

"To mention just a few among many other measures: states should list the Iranian Revolutionary Guard Corps, an organization that has been at the vanguard of the Islamic Republic's campaign of state terrorism, as a terrorist entity. An Argentinean judiciary's decision has led to Interpol arrest warrants against the perpetrators of the murders of many Israeli diplomats and Jews in Buenos Aires. These warrants should be enforced. Furthermore, civil suits should be instituted where appropriate against Iran and its terrorist agents for its perpetration of acts of terror. The principle of universal jurisdiction should be invoked to hold Iran's leaders—under indictment for war crimes and crimes against humanity—accountable.

"In the matter of Iran's systematic and widespread assaults on the human rights of its own people, governments, parliamentarians, media, NGOs, church leaders, trade unionists, academics, and many others should expose, unmask, and hold Iran accountable for its massive domestic repression. In that regard, US Senator Mark Kirk and I have established an Inter-Parliamentary Group for Human Rights in Iran. Our group has initiated the Global Iranian Political Prisoner Advocacy Program, calling on parliamentarians internationally to 'adopt' a political prisoner and create a critical mass of advocacy on behalf of these prisoners of conscience.

"Furthermore, all states should make major efforts to support dissidents directly by funding programs to help activists mobilize and circumvent electronic barriers. In addition, we must put pressure on satellite companies that carry Iranian state television, as the Iranian authorities use their airwaves not only to spread propaganda, but for televising coerced confessions and show trials as well." Cotler concludes: "There is no absence of remedies—some are political and some are diplomatic. Others are economic and legal. We need to internationalize the advocacy and invoke an integrated critical mass of remedy to counteract the intersecting critical mass of threat. Silence and indifference is not an option. The time to act is now."

Indoctrinating Palestinian Children to Genocidal Hatred: A Psychiatrist's Perspective

D R. DAPHNE BURDMAN, psychiatrist and pathologist, was assistant clinical professor of pathology at the State University of New York at Stony Brook and a lieutenant colonel in the US Army.

"In both the Palestinian Authority and the Hamas-ruled territory of Gaza there are carefully planned, widespread campaigns of incitement of children. Due to this indoctrination, children start even viewing positively their involvement in terrorist actions in which they risk their lives. This process of incitement should be better documented. Thereafter, it should be analyzed how this fits into the broader picture of Palestinian and Muslim genocidal ideology. Finally, methods of detoxifying brainwashed children should be discussed."

Burdman remarks: "This incitement process has been poorly covered by the international media. Thus, Westerners are largely ignorant of the sinister development of these profoundly 'successful' programs. These are based on both familiar and innovative techniques of persuasion and indoctrination. Similar ones were used to maximum effect by totalitarian regimes including Nazi Germany, the Soviet KGB, and Chinese intelligence services. There is increasing evidence that some of these sources have inspired and trained the Palestinian Authority.

"This incitement of Palestinian children has led to widespread hatred and an urge to violence. Palestinian leaders incite children to undertake such violent actions against Israelis even when it is likely that they will be injured or killed. They are promised to become martyrs who will be admired as heroes in Palestinian society and will find a place in Paradise with Allah. Thus encouraged, children's natural fears are reduced. They then desire to be in situations where they risk injury or even death.

"This mass indoctrination of children is based on a carefully planned campaign that draws on strongly held cultural beliefs and deep-seated psychological mechanisms. The incitement uses a multimodal methodology, preaching Palestinian nationalism, martyrology, and, under Hamas, emphasizing worldwide hegemonic Sharia. The campaign utilizes the media, schools, and the street, as well as religious figures.

"Indoctrination in the Palestinian areas is far broader than textbook and television sources, encompassing general societal elements including newsprint, parents, teachers, methods of teaching with encouragement and praise for adherence, and strong disapproval for less devoted students. Imams are extremely influential in successfully emphasizing the goals of jihad and martyrdom. Summer camps, and the naming of streets, playgrounds, and soccer teams for martyrs, help maintain the ambience throughout society.

"Among the psychological factors determining indoctrination, the transmission of emotion is the ultimate weapon. Hatred in this context is paramount, and abhorrence of the Jews, and to a lesser extent of the Americans, is transmitted. In patriarchal Palestinian society, manipulation of children's emotions thus draws on fear of displeasing Allah.

"Studies show that the frequent background drumbeat in the Palestinian Authority TV clips augments explosive states of physical tension and heightened suggestibility. This idea of conversion to self-destruction is a mystery for the Western mind.

"Hamas and Islamic Jihad hear from clerics in mosques about young-sters who seem particularly ready for martyrdom. These are then given a lengthy course of spiritual studies and military-type training. They are also taught that dying as a suicide bomber will open the doors to Paradise for themselves and their families.

"It is noteworthy that the suicide-bombing phenomenon tapered off considerably after March 2002, due both to the markedly more efficient prevention by IDF targeted killings and preemptive actions, and to the construction of the security fence in strategic locations. The policy of the Palestinian Authority was unchanged but became less and less successful."

When asked about the possibilities to detoxify Palestinian childrens' minds, Burdman says: "Even when violence between Palestinians and Israe-lis stops, Palestinian children's state of mind will not change by itself. Once one has been taught that suicide attacks will open the doors to Paradise for oneself and one's family, much more is needed for detoxification. The problem is all the more acute if one grows up in an authoritarian society where there is little if any independent thinking.

"Rectification of the martyrdom indoctrination will be lengthy and complex. From professional experience one learns that it is questionable whether it can be successful. The best that we can hope for is a gradual attrition of Palestinian indomitable nationalism and Islamist hegemonic hopes. In the absence of external forces this might be a possibility, but at the present time, with a rising crescendo of expressed international Islamist expansionism both violent and nonviolent, the immediate outlook appears bleak."

Jewish Middle Eastern Refugees Lost Far More Than Palestinian Refugees

S IDNEY ZABLUDOFF is an economist who worked for the White House, the CIA, and the Treasury Department for more than thirty years. Upon retirement in 1995, he focused mainly on issues related to the restitution of Jewish assets stolen during the Holocaust era.

"Roughly one million Jewish people became refugees when they were forced out of Middle Eastern and North African countries after 1948. Their ancestors had lived there for thousands of years in many cases. Before 1948, there were more than one million Jews in the Middle East and North Africa outside of the area that became Israel. The total number fell by half during the years following the 1948 war and then declined to some 100,000 following the 1967 conflict. The Jewish population fell further in the ensuing years and by 2012 amounted to just about 30,000.

"The exact number of Palestinians who fled Israel from November 1947 to December 1948 will never be known. The most plausible figure is some 550,000. To this one must add about 100,000 new refugees from the 1967 war, bringing the net total to 650,000. Thus the number of Jews forced to flee through the acts of the countries they lived in exceeded the original number of Palestinian refugees by more than 50 percent."

Zabludoff: "The difference in individual assets lost was even bigger. It should be noted that it is impossible to determine an exact value for asset losses, and arguments can be made for different asset values. The most solid estimate for assets given up by Palestinians fleeing the 1948 war was by John Measham Berncastle, who undertook the task in the early 1950s under the aegis of the newly formed United Nations Conciliation Commission for Palestine (UNCCP). His estimate was 120 million Palestinian pounds of which about 100 million was for land and buildings and 20 million for movable property. One might add another 5 million pounds for bank accounts.

"This total of 125 million Palestinian pounds amounted to $350 million in 1948. This is equal to some $650 per 1948–1949 refugee. This number seems reasonable when compared to similar data. For example, per capita assets for Eastern Europe during the late 1930s ranged from $550 to $700. These were the best equivalent asset statistics available. To this must be added the asset losses for those additional 100,000 Palestinians who fled in the aftermath of the 1967 war and the 40,000 internally displaced persons in Israel (IDPs). The latter are included even though they were often given new property and/or compensation. At a realistic $700 per capita, that would amount to another $100 million in lost Palestinian assets. Thus, the total of assets lost by Palestinians is some $450 million. In 2011 prices, this would amount to $4.2 billion.

"A comparable estimate of the assets lost by the Jews fleeing Middle East and North African countries is $6.5 billion at 2011 prices. There are two major reasons for the higher value of assets lost by Jewish refugees. First, the number of Jewish refugees is some 50 percent higher than that of Palestinian refugees. Second, the demographic nature of the two groups varied. A higher percentage of the Jewish population was urban, mainly traders and professionals, who would tend to accumulate more assets than the Palestine population, which was more rural.

"There are other considerations. A major unknown is community property such as hospitals, mosques, synagogues, and religious schools. One estimate put the value of such Jewish-owned property in Egypt at $600 million in 2011 dollars. It can be assumed that here also the Jewish amounts are larger than those of Palestinians because of the higher number of refugees and a larger number of locations.

"From a global perspective, the Palestinian refugee issue is unique. Since 1920, all other major refugee crises involving the exchange of religious or ethnic populations, while creating hardships, were dealt with in a single generation. Issues, such as right of return and compensation were never adequately resolved and were largely forgotten. As in the case of Jewish refugees from the Middle East and North Africa, all non-Palestinian refugees were absorbed into their new homeland. Such circumstances occurred in the case of Greek-Turkish and India-Pakistan disputes as well as the enormous number of refugees from the Second World War.

"For most refugee crises of the post-Second World War era, compensation came mainly in the form of temporary assistance and lasted only a few years while the refugees were becoming assimilated into their new surroundings. Only the Palestinian refugee issue has persisted for such a long time. The result is that during the past 62 years, UNRWA has spent some $18 billion (current prices) to support Palestinian refugees. This amount is considerably more than the assets these refugees lost.

"In comparison, examples of compensation falling short are numerous. Less than 20 percent of asset losses by Jews in Nazi-occupied Europe have been returned, despite the fact that the Holocaust was an event unequaled in modern history—the extermination of more than two-thirds of continental European Jewry. This is the reality we face."

The Powerful Saudi Lobby
in the United States

D R. MITCHELL G. BARD is executive director of the nonprofit
American-Israeli Cooperative Enterprise (AICE). He is also
director of the Jewish Virtual Library, the world's most comprehensive
online encyclopedia of Jewish history and culture. Bard has published
more than twenty books, the latest one being *The Arab Lobby*.

*"Israel's enemies have consistently claimed that a powerful Israeli lobby in the
United States acts contrary to American interests. In truth, the Israeli lobby
reflects the views of the American people while the little known Arab lobby works
largely unseen to undermine American's interests, values, and security.*

*"This lobby's components are heterogeneous. One element is the diplomats from
the 21 Arab countries and those of a number of non–Arab Islamic nations. Others
are US defense contractors, former American government officials employed by
Arab states, corporations with business interests in the Middle East, a number of
human rights NGOs, and the United Nations. To this one should add numerous
academics—mainly from Middle East studies departments—members of the media
and cultural elite, several non-evangelical Christian groups, as well as American
Arabs and Muslims. By far the most potent Arab lobbyists, however, are the Saudis."*
Bard remarks: "Arab lobbies have no significant grassroots support. They
therefore operate in a different way from AIPAC, the main American

organization defending Israel's interests. The Saudi lobby mainly takes a 'top-down approach.' Its principal concern is to ensure that the heads of the royal family stay on their shoulders, so, while it pays lip service to the Palestinian issue, it is the survival of the House of Saud that matters most.

"The Saudis have almost unlimited financial resources, which they use to reward former officials in hopes of influencing those still in office. As Prince Bandar, a former Saudi ambassador to the United States, once said, if the Saudis get a reputation for taking care of their friends when they leave office, you'd be surprised how much better friends you have who are just coming into office.

"The former government officials can guide the Saudis on how to manipulate US policy makers. They can use the contacts they have developed during their government career to gain Saudi access to decision makers. As the media often call on them to comment on Middle East affairs as nonpartisan experts, they also act as Saudi propagandists.

"Many American policy makers think that the United States depends on the Saudis because they regulate the world oil market. Thus a Faustian relationship has developed between the two countries. The Saudis sell oil to the United States in return for America protecting the Saudi regime. The Saudis also act like drug pushers manipulating the US addiction to oil. The price is kept high enough to make huge profits, but low enough to discourage significant investments in alternative sources of energy.

"Clark Clifford, who was Truman's political adviser, realized the United States did not need to give in to Saudi blackmail. He said in 1948: 'The Arab states must have oil royalties or go broke. Their need of the United States is greater than our need of them.'

"Throughout the history of the US-Saudi relationship, presidents were in a position to demand support for American policies in exchange for the security umbrella keeping the Saud family in power, but, they did not. Even after US forces saved the kingdom during the first Iraq War in 1991,

President Bush was unwilling to seek Saudi support in promoting peace between the Palestinians and Israel.

"In addition to undermining the US interest in peace, the Saudis undermine American values by maintaining one of the world's most repressive societies that has historically discriminated against women, Jews, Christians, and even its Shiite Muslim minority.

"The Saudis have also not been helpful to President Barack Obama in promoting his peace plans. They were not willing to make a single concession to Israel when he asked them to do so in recent years. Yet Obama agreed to a major supply of arms to Saudi Arabia. There are similar examples from the past. President Jimmy Carter asked the Saudis in vain to support the Camp David agreements in 1978. After he was rebuffed, he still sold arms to the kingdom.

"The Saudis are also terror supporters in many ways. Long before 9/11, Saudi Arabia was a major funder of the PLO's international terror campaign. The United States, however, looked the other way. The American public never understood the Saudi role in terrorism until 9/11. Then it became known that 15 of the 19 hijackers were Saudis. As we learned from WikiLeaks and other sources, the Saudis are the leading supporters of terror. As Stuart Levey, the undersecretary of the Treasury in charge of tracking terror financing, said: 'If I could somehow snap my fingers and cut off the funding from one country, it would be Saudi Arabia.'

"The Saudi lobby thus works in many ways against US interests. The more this is exposed, the better it will be for both the United States and democracy at large."

Where European Anti-Americanism
and Anti-Semitism Meet

ANDREI S. MARKOVITS is the Karl W. Deutsch Collegiate Professor of Comparative Politics and German Studies at the University of Michigan in Ann Arbor. He came to the United States in 1960, but spent the bulk of his teenage years in Vienna before returning to New York in 1967 to attend Columbia University where he received all five of his university degrees.

"Israeli psychiatrist Zvi Rex was correct in saying that the Germans will never forgive the Jews for Auschwitz. In an analogous manner, I would argue that Western Europeans will also never forgive the Americans for being daily reminders that it was the Americans—together with the Red Army—who defeated Nazism, and not the Europeans themselves.

"Anti-Semitism in Europe goes back a thousand years. Anti-Americanism as a discourse and an ideology emerged more than 200 years ago among European elites. America and Jews are seen by many Europeans as paragons of a modernity they dislike and distrust: money-driven, profit-hungry, urban, universalistic, individualistic, mobile, rootless, inauthentic, and thus hostile to established traditions and values. Anti-Americanism and anti-Semitism are the only major icons shared by the European extreme Left and far Right, including neo-Nazis."

Markovits says: "It continues to remain unclear what emotional ties and

THIS IS TIRESOME THEY ARE ALL SOCIALISTS

emotive identities Europeans share. One need not have to be witness of the crises concerning the euro to notice that the solidarity between Germans and Greeks is rather low. But one important characteristic that both Germans and Greeks share is their not being American. No identity has ever emerged without an important counter-identity. Anti-Americanism thus enables Europeans to create a hitherto missing European identity that must emerge if the European project is to succeed. The effusive initial praise of Obama by Europeans in no way excludes the antipathies harbored by Europeans toward America, which received unprecedented amplification and legitimacy during the Bush presidency. Indeed, by rendering Obama into a quasi European, the Europeans' superficial affection for Obama coexisted perfectly with their continued disdain for America.

"Anti-Americanism and anti-Semitism relate to each other and empirically are almost always in close proximity. The overlap in bias between them has become more pronounced since the end of the Second World War. Both are 'isms' which indicate they are institutionalized and commonly used as a modern ideology. As such, their discourses have their own semantics.

"While the two European prejudices overlap, there are also huge differences. Anti-Semitism has killed millions of people, while European anti-Americanism has only murdered a few, if that many. There were never any pogroms against Americans. Violence, as a rule, did not go further than the destruction of property and the burning of many American flags. There has never been a blood libel about Americans.

"Another major difference is that of power. Since the nineteenth century, America has become an increasingly powerful country. Its military might was very influential in the First World War and was powerful well before then. The Jews only had power in the warped imagination of their enemies.

"Israel, however, after the 1967 Six-Day War, became increasingly perceived as being far more powerful than it actually was. The image of the strong and tough Jew emerged and similarities with the Americans increased in the perception of many Europeans. By dint of identifying Israel as this omnipotent entity, Europeans could openly resent it and resorted to characterizations of Israel's essence and its very existence with rather similar terms and tones that resembled old-fashioned European anti-Semitism.

"The powerless Arabs are now presented as the victims of the powerful Jews. One expression of European anti-Semitism is that the Jews—who should have been victims—are seen as perpetrators. As far as Israel is concerned, there is an additional dimension that is not prima facie relevant to anti-Americanism. Europe has a major unresolved relationship with its past. The constant analogizing of Israelis with Nazis comes from the European gut. By doing this, Europeans absolve themselves of their own history. At the same time, they succeed in accusing their former victims of behaving like their worst perpetrators.

"No other vaguely comparable conflict has attained in Europe anywhere near the shrillness and acuity as has the Israeli-Palestinian conflict; not the mass murders in Chechnya, not the ones in the many post-Yugoslav wars, and not the murders of Muslims at the hands of Serbs and Croats.

"Since the Second World War—and especially since the ascent of the New Left in the late 1960s—left-wing anti-Semitism has remained conveniently veiled by anti-Zionism. However, the European Left's hatred of Israel has become much more potent over the last 15–20 years for one crucial reason: it is the Left's language and discourse—not the Right's—that have been adopted by the European mainstream.

"If one were to list the major icons that defined the core of what it means to be left wing these days, to be a progressive, there is no doubt that an active antipathy toward Israel and the United States would be on this list. Most likely both enmities would hover around the top of the list rather than its bottom. The sad fact is that a dislike of and disdain for Israel

having a false piety in lieu of

and the United States have become as essential to being a progressive as are income redistribution, the defense of workers' rights, the protection of the environment, advocacy on behalf of gays and lesbians, and feminism."

Judaic Christian faith. in God.

Non-Governmental Organizations against Israel

P ROFESSOR GERALD STEINBERG teaches political science and international relations at Bar Ilan University. He has headed NGO Monitor since its founding in 2002. It is the only independent research framework which systematically examines the claims, and challenges the power of the NGO political network.

"Among Israel's many attackers, non-governmental organizations (NGOs) are the least subject to external monitoring. These anti-Israel NGOs claim to promote human rights and humanitarian aid, yet are characterized by a lack of professionalism and a postcolonial ideological agenda. In some cases, theological anti-Semitism is an additional factor.

"The research organization NGO Monitor has documented anti-Israel acts for a number of major NGOs in detail. This includes the Israel-related activities of Amnesty International, Human Rights Watch, Oxfam, Christian Aid, and many other organizations."

Steinberg says: "One can monitor the bias of NGOs objectively. One quantitative method is counting the number of pages, individual reports, press conferences, and other similar measures over the past decade devoted to various subjects. The research shows a huge discrepancy between the frequent condemnations of Israel and lesser attention paid to closed dictatorial regimes, or to other countries involved in violent conflicts.

"There are also qualitative methods. Anti-Israel NGOs prefer to use a certain language to attack Israel. This includes terms such as 'war crimes,' 'collective punishment,' 'impunity,' and so on. They use these much less against other countries. This highlights the violation of universal principles of human rights by these NGOs.

"Groups such as Amnesty International, Human Rights Watch (HRW), Oxfam, and various church-based international aid groups based in Europe are very well funded. They therefore exercise much political power. These NGOs are also the worst offenders of the moral principles they falsely claim to promote. HRW hired people to run its Middle East and North Africa division who are profoundly stained by a history of crude anti-Israel bias. NGO Monitor has documented this frequently.

"These NGOs have taken over major international platforms in the spheres of human rights and humanitarian aid. Many European governments outsource these activities by providing large sums of money, with little supervision over private 'charities' and NGOs. In addition, journalists, academics, and other members of the 'foreign policy elite' are often closely involved with such organizations, or accept their claims and agendas without question. In 2002, Amnesty 'expert' Derek Pounder told the BBC that he could confirm a huge Jenin 'massacre' committed by the Israeli Defense Forces. The myth he created was only exposed after it had been repeated hundreds of times and the damage to Israel was done.

"Furthermore, diplomats and politicians in the United Nations often abdicate their responsibility in dealing with complex human rights claims to NGOs. They rely on them for drafts of speeches, reports, and other services. One particularly egregious case was the 2009 Goldstone Report on the Gaza War. Journalists often tend to copy NGO press releases without any independent examination of the factual claims or pseudolegal arguments.

"In the most blatant cases of NGO bias against Israel, there are four factors. First, officials at the head of international NGOs are often tainted by a strong anti-Western postcolonial ideology. Since 1967, they have assigned Israel to the nationalist and capitalist Western camp, which is, by definition, guilty. A second reason why NGOs focus on the Israeli-Palestinian conflict is that it is ever-present in the media. This helps their marketing strategy by giving them visibility in the competition for funds and influence.

"A third factor is that the UN Human Rights Council in Geneva is controlled by Arab and Islamic blocs. To be seen as having influence there, NGOs must toe the 'political line,' which means an intense anti-Israel position. The fourth factor is classic Christian theological anti-Semitism and replacement theology. These are prominent in UK-based NGOs such as War on Want, Christian Aid, and Amnesty. They are also found in the activities of church-based humanitarian aid groups in Scandinavia and Ireland.

"These powerful organizations are difficult to defeat. Yet NGO Monitor has shown in a number of important cases that success is possible. To mention a few examples: In 2009, our detailed refutation of unfounded NGO allegations at the core of the Goldstone Report led its author to disavow his own publication. HRW founder Robert Bernstein denounced this organization after NGO Monitor systematically exposed the deeply biased agenda of its Middle East and North Africa Division and HRW's efforts to raise money from members of the Saudi elite while ignoring that regime's severe human rights abuses.

"Furthermore, NGO Monitor's reports on the destructive contribution from funders of these organizations—such as the New Israel Fund and European governments—have led them to gradually end their support for the most egregious NGOs involved in boycott, divestment, and sanctions (BDS) as well as other hate-based activities against Israel. Similar monitoring is or could be applied to many other Israel-hate organizations outside of the NGO field."

A Journal on Anti-Semitism
Born out of Adversity

S TEVEN BAUM is a clinical psychologist who has been in private practice for over thirty years. He teaches periodically and publishes articles, essays, and books. A number of them deal with anti-Semitism and genocide.

"My negative experiences with American and British editors who were biased against Israel led to the creation of the Journal for the Study of Antisemitism *(JSA) in 2008. I did this together with my friend Neal Rosenberg. It has become a periodical where articles can be published, without giving in to the prevailing anti-Israel rhetoric."*

Baum says: "I started off in the field of aging and adult development—the study of stages of psychological changes that occur as we age. I soon became fascinated with the Holocaust and other genocides. I later realized that it was the psychology of anti-Semitism that remained elusive and for the last ten years, focused my attention on why people hate Jews."

Baum relates some of his experiences: "I carried out a study on hundred North American Muslims and hundred Christians who were given tests on the topics of anti-Semitism and other psychological phenomena. Their scores were then added up regarding levels and types of anti-Semitic beliefs.

The results were that mainstream Christian anti-Semitism scores were low, while most Muslim scores were high. Threat to one's social identity emerged as the strongest predictors of anti-Semitism in the Muslim samples.

"I sent my study to the *Journal of Contemporary Religion*. Its editor said that a reviewer wanted me to explain those religious differences in terms of Israel's policy toward the Palestinians. I replied that 1,500 years of anti-Semitic Muslim culture were the most likely source. The editor said that she would not publish the article until this issue was resolved with the reviewer.

"I decided to insert a sentence that had no bearing on anything, yet highlighted *context* instead of anti-Semitic culture and wrote: 'Context is equally important to consider. For instance, the survey was conducted shortly after the July 7, 2005 bombings in London and the backdrop of violence may have polarized viewpoints, increasing the anti-Israel sentiment and anti-Semitism ratings among Muslim youth.' I gave a source which supported this. The journal then published the study in 2008. Most people understand, however, that Jews and Israel have nothing to do with the London subway bombings.

"Around the same time, Cambridge University Press was preparing to publish my book *Psychology of Genocide*. The line editor challenged me on anything critical of Islam. He asked questions such as 'how can you say anything negative about jihad—it is one of the pillars of Islam?' I said that despite that fact, it had become a call for genocide. I complained to the main editor and, thereafter, there were few further political challenges.

"The same publisher had an option for my next book *Antisemitism Explained*. Its main theme was that when one makes enough negative and false statements about Jews—or any other group—a tipping point is reached and people accept the anti-Semitic fallacy as true. I offered evidence of how this worked and paralleled the process to advertising psychology. Cambridge Press's editors liked the idea. One chapter explained how Muslim propaganda had affected hatred of Israel along the same lines.

"The new editor of Cambridge Press whom I dealt with didn't like this explanation of the anti-Israel sentiment, even though it was consistent with the main theme of my book. He wanted me to focus on *context*, i.e., the Palestinian point of view. I asked what this had to do with a book on anti-Semitism. The reply came down to 'fix it or walk.' I did not want to distort my opinions, whereupon the editor rejected my book.

"I then searched for another publisher for three years. I finally found University Press of America—an imprint of Rowman and Littlefield— which published it in 2012.

"Several other academics told me that they had a difficult time publishing articles which put Israel in a favorable light. I realized then that there were no academic journals which were specifically devoted to investigating anti-Semitism. Pro-Palestinian academics, however, encountered no such problems. By contrast there is a *Journal of Palestinian Studies* which is available in many libraries."

Baum remarks: "The biannual *Journal for the Study of Antisemitism* is entering its fifth year. It has a respectable board of editors. The original footnoted articles in it are peer-reviewed. Guest editors have dealt with issues devoted to themes such as Eastern Europe, Law and anti-Semitism, and Campus anti-Semitism. These are global phenomena. Another issue addressed anti-Semitism in Latin America.

"Some authors of essays and book reviews the JSA publishes would have difficulty placing them elsewhere. The journal is self-funded and not affiliated academically. Despite these odds, it gives a voice to Jewish and Israeli encounters with hatred. One could conclude that my negative experiences have led to a positive end result."

Christian Friends and Foes of Israel

D AVID R. PARSONS is media director for the International Christian Embassy Jerusalem, senior producer of the weekly radio program *Front Page Jerusalem*, and contributing editor of *The Jerusalem Post Christian Edition*. From 1991 to 1995 he served as general counsel for CIPAC, a Christian pro-Israeli lobby registered with Congress to advocate for strong US-Israel relations.

"The Holocaust brought about a major change in thinking about the Jewish people in many Christian circles. It was a huge moral shock that, in the heart of Christian Europe, a genocide had taken place that aimed to annihilate the Jews. To many it was clear that centuries of Christian anti-Semitic teachings had paved the way for the mass murders by the Nazis and their supporters. These crimes alone, however, could not have shifted the theological thinking of many Christians to such a large extent. Many would still have said: 'The Shoah is yet one more example that the Jews are forever cursed.'"

Parsons observes: "It was the theological shock of the creation of the State of Israel in 1948 that challenged fundamental church teachings and doctrine concerning the Jewish people. For centuries the Christian mainstream thought that the Jews, who were blamed for killing Christ, were doomed to endless wanderings. Accordingly, they had been dispersed around the world, never to return to the Land of Israel or play an important role in God's redemptive plan for humanity. With the birth of the Church, the Jews had served their purpose once and for all.

"Then after the Second World War, rather suddenly Jewish sovereignty was restored in the Land of Israel. This development didn't square with mainstream Christian doctrines. Thereupon several Christian churches, of which the large Catholic Church is a good example, gradually steered their institutions toward new attitudes concerning the Jewish people.

"However, there also remain Christians who have refused to change their doctrines to fit this new reality of a restored Israel. They would rather try to retool the facts to fit their classic theology of a rejected Israel. This is perhaps a little-known but large motivating factor for many pro-Palestinian Christians in the Western world.

"They would like to whittle Israel back to a binational state of two peoples, Jews and Arabs, and three religions: Islam, Judaism, and Christianity. This is an important source of the Christian involvement in the divestment campaigns, apartheid branding of Israel, and other anti-Israeli efforts. Although this activism has an underlying theological basis, it is also part of the wider 'culture wars' between Left and Right.

"Replacement theology, also called Supersessionism, is the main theology of Israel's Christian foes. It is based on the idea that God's unique relationship with the Church is the replacement or the completion of the promises made to the Jewish people, and thus Israel's 'election' no longer stands. Palestinian liberation theology uses Jesus as a historic role model, identifying with him as the 'first Palestinian revolutionary.' Thus it justifies Palestinian violence against Israelis as acceptable acts of the oppressed against the oppressor.

"Within the pro-Israeli Protestant camp there are two major theological schools. The first is covenantal Christian theology, which is based on the belief that God eternally keeps his covenantal promises made through Abraham, Moses, David, and Jesus. We believe the Hebrew prophets were servants of the covenants and tell us something about how God will keep his covenantal promises. The foundation of our pro-Israeli stance, however, is the Abrahamic covenant. The people in the International Christian Embassy belong to this theological school. The second is Dispensationalism, which says that Israel was temporarily replaced by the Church but—at the end of days —Israel will once again be God's main redemptive agent in the world.

"Today there are more Christian Zionists than ever. The Protestant evangelicals number perhaps as many as 600 million today — these are people who claim to have had a 'born again' experience and who view the Bible as the inspired Word of God. The Evangelical stream is the fastest-growing religious movement in the world. The Chinese government recently admitted that there are as many as 120 million evangelical Christians in their country, more than the number of Communist Party members. Many millions of evangelical Christians have a compelling love for Israel and the Jewish people. Every year, about eight thousand Christians come from nearly a hundred countries to participate in the celebration of the biblical Feast of Tabernacles in Jerusalem."

Parsons concludes: "Jews can challenge Christian adversaries on the facts, on history, and so on. But Israel and world Jewry would be well advised to stay out of the theological debates among Christians, since some will not take Jews seriously because they do not accept the New Testament as scripture. The theological battles over Israel will have to be fought out within the Christian world and not elsewhere."

The Anti-Israeli Policies
of the World Council of Churches

DEXTER VAN ZILE is Christian Media Analyst for the Committee for Accuracy in Middle East Reporting in America (CAMERA). His writings have appeared in numerous American Jewish newspapers, as well as in *The Jerusalem Post*, *Ecumenical Trends*, and *The Boston Globe*.

"The World Council of Churches, an umbrella organization for 349 Protestant and Orthodox churches founded in 1948, has been largely hostile to Israel, particularly during times of conflict. WCC institutions demonize Israel, use a double-standard to assess its actions, and from time to time delegitimize the Jewish state. They have also persistently denied the intent of Israel's adversaries to deprive the Jewish people of their right to a sovereign state.

"The WCC's use of double standards against Israel is frequent. When it condemns Israel, the WCC speaks loudly and unequivocally about the 'terrible' things done by the Jewish state. When one of Israel's neighbors does something much worse, the WCC descends into pious incomprehensibility that leaves readers wondering exactly who did what to whom?"

Van Zile says that a few among many examples over the decades are representative of the WCC's recurrent anti-Israelism: "The WCC's response to events in Lebanon in the 1970s and 1980s was simple. In their declarations, the WCC failed to hold the PLO accountable for its actions, but vociferously condemned Israel. It offered vague and diffuse condemnations of massacres in Lebanon in those decades, failing to provide details about either the identity of the victims or the identity and motives of the perpetrators. Yet when Israel invaded Lebanon in 1982, WCC institutions forcefully condemned Israel, while attributing malign intent to it.

"The Middle East Council of Churches has prevailed upon the WCC to condemn Israel. On the other hand, the Russian Orthodox Church was able to prevent the WCC from condemning the Soviet invasion of Afghanistan in the 1980s.

"In 2005, the WCC's Central Committee expressed support for the anti-Israeli divestment campaign in mainline American Protestant churches. After the Presbyterian Church (USA's) General Assembly passed a divestment resolution which stated that Israel's 'occupation' was at the root of violence against innocents on both sides of the conflict—as if anti-Semitic incitement in Palestinian society had nothing to do with the conflict—the WCC's Central Committee issued a minute lauding the decision. 'This action is commendable in both method and manner, uses criteria rooted in faith, and calls on members to do the things that make for peace (Luke 19:42).'

"In June 2010, WCC General Secretary Olav Fykse Tveit issued a public statement lamenting the confrontation that took place between Israeli commandos and passengers on board the *Mavi Marmara*, part of the Free Gaza Movement's flotilla, which attempted to bring Turkish-trained jihadists into the Gaza Strip using Western peace activists as cover.

"Tveit mischaracterized the events, writing: 'We condemn the assault and killing of innocent people who were attempting to deliver humanitarian assistance to the people of Gaza, who have been under a crippling Israeli blockade since 2007.' Tveit went on to denounce 'the flagrant violation of international law by Israel in attacking and boarding a humanitarian convoy in international waters.'This was a lie, as international law permitted Israel to act as it did.

"The WCC has even established two bodies—the Ecumenical Accompaniment Programme in Palestine and Israel (EAPPI) and the Palestine Israel Ecumenical Forum (PIEF)—with the singular purpose of ending Israel's 'occupation' of the West Bank and the Gaza Strip. There is nothing similar concerning any other country.

"The WCC's attitude on the persecution of Coptic Christians in their homeland of Egypt is radically different. Copts have been subjected to mob violence and their churches have been burned on a regular basis. They are demonized on television and the Internet by Muslim extremists, accused of kidnapping Muslim women and forcing them to convert to Christianity when in fact Coptic women and girls have been raped and abducted and forced to convert to Islam by their neighbors.

"The WCC has expressed its worry about the situation of the Copts in Egypt. What is remarkable, however, is the absence of any condemnation of the Supreme Council of the Armed Forces—which governs Egypt—for failing to protect Coptic Christians. It also does not speak in a forthright manner about what is happening. Neither do the National Council of Churches in the United States, nor any of the mainline Protestant churches in the United States that have assailed Israel so frequently and so vociferously in the past few years.

"One conclusion is inescapable: The WCC's obsession with Israel, claiming that it is the source of all the troubles in the Middle East, has made it impossible for the organization to address an ongoing campaign of religious cleansing perpetrated by Muslim extremists against Christians in Muslim-majority countries in the Middle East and elsewhere. Consequently, these Muslims can engage in a slow, grinding campaign to eliminate Christianity from the Middle East without effective challenge from the World Council of Churches."

Muslims Drive out Christians from Palestinian Territories

Justus Reid Weiner is an international human rights lawyer and a member of the Israel and New York Bar Associations. His professional publications have appeared in leading law journals and intellectual magazines. Weiner lectures widely abroad and in Israel and teaches international law and business courses at the Hebrew University of Jerusalem.

In Weiner's view, the crimes committed against Christian Arabs result from a way of thinking that dates back to the earliest days of Islam. "Traditionally, Christians and Jews were given an inferior social status known as *dhimmitude* in Islam. To this day, Muslim attitudes toward Christians and Jews are influenced by the concepts and prejudices that dhimmitude has spawned in Islamic society. The widespread persecution of Christians in various Muslim-dominated lands brings many proofs of this."

"The disputed territories of the West Bank and the Gaza Strip have been administered by the Palestinian Authority (PA) and in more recent years, in part, by Hamas. Under these regimes, the resident Christian Arabs have been victims of frequent human rights abuses including intimidation, beatings, land theft, firebombing of churches and other Christian institutions, denial of

employment, economic boycott, torture, kidnapping, forced marriage, sexual harassment, and extortion.

"Muslims who have converted to Christianity are the ones in the greatest danger. They are often left defenseless against cruelty by Muslim fundamentalists. PA and Hamas officials are directly responsible for many of the human rights violations. Christian Arabs also fall victim to the semi-anarchy that typifies PA rule."

Weiner: "Israel is the only exception in the Middle East where the Christian population since 1948 has increased. It has risen by more than 400 percent. This also includes non-Arab Christians, such as Russian Christians who have moved to Israel as spouses of Jews.

"As *dhimmis*, Christians living in Palestinian-controlled territories are subjected to debilitating legal, political, cultural, and religious restrictions. Muslim groups like Hamas and Islamic Jihad have built a culture of hatred upon the age-old foundations of Islamic society. Moreover, the PA has adopted Islamic law into its draft constitution.

"In such an environment, Christian Arabs have found themselves victims of prejudice and hate crimes. Tens of thousands of Palestinian Christians have left their ancestral homes and emigrated. They flee to almost any country that will issue them a visa.

"The demographics in the Palestinian areas have changed drastically. In Bethlehem, the Christian population was an 80 percent majority in 1950. Today, the population of Christian Arabs in Bethlehem is hovering at about 15 percent of the city's total population. Neither the Palestinian Christian leaders nor the PA want to reveal accurate statistics. That would mean the extent of the emigration would become publicly known. They would then have to face questions about the reasons for this decline."

Weiner points out that Yasser Arafat determined the policy that led to this demographic shift. "After the PA gained control of Bethlehem, it redistricted the municipal boundaries of the city. Arafat also defied tradition by appointing a Muslim governor of the city. The Bethlehem City Council, which by Palestinian law must have a Christian majority, has been taken over by Muslims. Eight of the fifteen seats on the Council are still reserved for Christians, but Hamas controls the City Council with some Christian allies. Arafat crowned his efforts when he converted the Greek Orthodox monastery next to the Church of Nativity into his official Bethlehem residence.

"The problems for Christians in Bethlehem are typical throughout the Middle East. As in Palestinian society, Christian Arabs have no voice and no protection. It is no wonder they have been leaving. Because of emigration—some of it dating back two or three generations—seventy percent of Christian Arabs who originally resided in the West Bank and Gaza now live abroad. Tens of thousands live in Sydney, Berlin, Santiago, Detroit, and Toronto. The emigration of Christian Arabs has multiplied over the last decade, with no end in sight.

"It is currently estimated that the number of Christians living in Gaza totals only 1,500–3,000 amid 1.2 million Muslims. Probably less than fifty thousand Christians remain in all of East Jerusalem, the West Bank, and Gaza together."

Weiner concludes: "The human rights crimes against the Christian Arabs in the disputed territories are committed by Muslims. Yet many Palestinian Christian leaders accuse Israel of these crimes rather than the actual perpetrators. These patriarchs and archbishops of Christian Arab denominations obfuscate the truth and put their own people in danger. This is often for personal benefit or due to intimidation. This motif has been adopted by a variety of Christian leaders in the Western world. Others who are aware of the human rights crimes choose to remain silent about them."

Protestants and Israel:
The Kairos Document Debate 2009

P ROFESSOR HANS JANSEN is the author of a major and frequently reprinted work in Dutch titled *Christian Theology after Auschwitz*. The subtitle of his first tome is *The History of 2000 Years of Church Anti-Semitism*. The second tome—in two volumes—is subtitled *The Roots of Anti-Semitism in the New Testament*. Jansen, a Dutch Protestant, taught history at the Flemish Free University in Brussels (1990–2000) and since 2002, teaches at the Simon Wiesenthal Institute in the same town.

"The Protestant world is greatly divided regarding Israel. On one hand, there is much hate promotion against Israel, on the other hand, there are many supporters of Israel, in particular among Evangelical and Orthodox Protestants.

"One important occasion where both could be seen was at the debate concerning a text which became known as the Kairos document. It was published in 2009 by Palestinian Christians. The official title is 'A moment of truth: A word of faith, hope and love from the heart of Palestinian suffering.'"

Jansen: "The central argument of the Kairos document is that only Israel is responsible for the problems in the region. The document called for considering the Israeli occupation policy as 'a sin.' The main aim of the document is to call for an international economic boycott against Israel.

"Later it became known that the Kairos document had been promoted in various countries as a declaration of the most prominent Palestinian Christian leaders such as the Greek Orthodox, the Roman Catholics, the Lutherans, the Anglicans, and the Baptists. This was entirely false—not a single leader of these churches signed the document.

"The document had been signed by only one church leader, Monib Younan, bishop of the Evangelical Lutheran Church in Jordan and the Holy Land. He later retracted his signature. This church has a few hundred members in the areas under the bishop's authority and was founded in 1959 by German Lutheran missionaries. Its membership is miniscule compared to the 400,000 Christians who live in these areas.

"Another initiator of the document is Yusef Dahan, local representative of the World Council of Churches. All other signatories are local pastors, laypeople, or religious functionaries who only represent themselves. One of them is the retired Roman Catholic Patriarch of Jerusalem, Michel Sabbah. His successor, the actual Patriarch, did not sign. Another signatory is the Greek Orthodox religious functionary Atallah Hanah, who is in discord with the Patriarch of his church.

"In many countries, the media has greatly overstated the relevance of the signatories. It has also understated the importance of the major opposition against the document.

"I have in particular followed the debate in the Netherlands. The Kairos document was criticized by various important Christian organizations. Twelve prominent theologians strongly attacked the document a few days after it was presented in December 2009 to leaders of Dutch churches. The Dutch media, however, gave the false impression that by accepting the document, the Dutch churches agreed with its content. This was untrue because how can one agree with a large document which one hasn't even read? The acceptance only meant that one was willing to listen to what needy Christians elsewhere had to say. Already at the acceptance meeting, there was criticism from the secretary of the by far largest Protestant community, The Protestant Churches of the Netherlands.

"The criticism of the theologians, which despite their eminence got little press coverage, was very broad. They called the document, 'the hour of misleading' and wrote that the Kairos document did not mention the promises God had given to Israel as a people in the Hebrew Bible. The document was even totally lacking in the biblical vision of Israel as a people. They heavily criticized the signatories because they used the Bible to legitimize their political preferences and visions. The theologians said that this approach turns religion into 'a human ideology.' They further remarked that 'the Kairos document is inspired by so-called new historians in the Middle East, who have for several years been re-writing the history of the 1948 events in favor of the Palestinians. These theologians referred to the document as 'a shameless brutality.'"

Jansen remarks: "Furthermore, the Kairos document is based on the so-called 'replacement theology,' which teaches that God's promise to the Jews has been passed on to the Christians. This theology has led to repeated persecution of Jews throughout the centuries. There are still many churches, especially in the Middle East, that support this ugly theology."

Jansen concludes: "From an historic perspective, it is important that the Kairos debate proves that when hatred of Judaism is nowadays propagated by Christians, there is also Christian opposition. Whoever studies the long history of this hatred finds that strong reactions against it in Christian circles were rare. From that point of view, the situation today is much more encouraging."

The Psychology of Jews
Who Embrace Their Enemies

Kenneth Levin is a psychiatrist, historian, and author of several books, among which is *The Oslo Syndrome: Delusions of a People under Siege*. He is a clinical instructor in psychiatry at Harvard Medical School.

In *The Oslo Syndrome*, Levin explains the attitude of Israeli self-haters: [There is] "a wish to believe Israel is in control of profoundly stressful circumstances over which, unfortunately, it has no real control. Genuine peace will come to the Middle East when the Arab world, by far the dominant party in the region, perceives such a peace as in its interest. Israeli policies have, in fact, very little impact on Arab perceptions in this regard, much less than the dynamics of domestic politics in the Arab states and of inter-Arab rivalries."

"A number of Jews and Israelis embrace criticism coming from anti-Semites and extreme anti-Israelis. They have many precursors in the lengthy history of the Jewish Diaspora.

"This phenomenon reveals great similarity, at the level of human psychology, to the response of children subjected to chronic abuse. Such children tend to blame themselves for their suffering. In their helpless condition, they have two alternatives. They can either acknowledge they are being unfairly victimized and reconcile

themselves to being powerless, or they can blame themselves for their predicament. The attraction of the latter—'I suffer because I am bad'—is that it serves the desire of being in control, fantasies that becoming 'good' will elicit a more benign response from their tormentors. Both children and adults invariably seek to avoid hopelessness."

Levin adds now: "Popular hatred for Israel, which is fanned by Arab governments, education systems, media, and Muslim clerics, runs deep in Arab opinion. This is not a totally isolated phenomenon, but fits into a much broader framework. Since the earliest days of the existence of the Arab-Muslim world, there has been widespread animosity against both religious and ethnic minorities in the region. It would be a mistake to attribute, for instance, the pressure on Christian minorities exclusively to the rise of Islamic fundamentalism. Popular Muslim-Arab hostility has also led to pressures on non-Arab Muslims such as the Berber populations in North Africa.

"While those Jews and Israelis who embrace anti-Jewish arguments typically do so in the hope of ingratiating themselves with the Jews' enemies, they will rarely acknowledge this motive. Rather, they typically claim that their position reflects a higher moral or ethical position.

"In the past and present, a common claim by anti-Semites has been that Jews are interested exclusively in their own well-being. This has led many Jews to focus their energies on broader social causes, even as the Jewish community suffered unique disabilities. Jews who take this course typically do not admit they are doing so to avoid being accused of Jewish parochialism. Rather, they claim to be righteously transcending narrow concerns to address more universal needs.

"During the Second World War, particularly after the Nazi extermination program was revealed in late 1942, many American Jewish leaders sought to raise public awareness of the plight of Europe's Jews and promote rescue efforts. Yet they also limited their campaign out of fear of arousing public anger over Jewish concern with a Jewish issue, and they often rationalized their doing so as reflecting devotion to the greater patriotic task of winning the war. It was largely non-Jewish voices which insisted the Nazi extermination program was not only a crime against the Jews but a crime against civilization and all of humanity and therefore should be of concern to everyone."

Levin observes: "In the last sixty years, the American Jewish community at large has energetically embraced support for Israel. This has been made much easier by the fact that the wider American public has traditionally been sympathetic toward the Jewish state.

"On the other hand, Israel has come under much criticism in certain American media, on many American campuses, and in several mainstream liberal churches. Those segments of the Jewish community who live and work in environments hostile to Israel, commonly embrace the anti-Israel bias around them. And they often insist they are being virtuous by doing so.

"The psychological dynamics of communities under attack explain why, both abroad and in Israel, the virtual siege placed upon the Jewish state will continue to lead segments of Jewish communities to support the besiegers and to urge Jewish self-reform as the path to winning relief. Yet the path they advocate is no less delusional than that of abused children who blame themselves for the abuse they experience. All too often such children doom themselves psychologically to lives of self-abnegation and misery. In the case of Jews indicting Israel for the hatred directed against it, the misery they cultivate goes far beyond themselves, and ultimately, undermines Israel's very survival."

The Communalities of Holocaust Deniers and Anti-Zionists

ELHANAN YAKIRA is Schulman Professor of Philosophy at the Hebrew University in Jerusalem. He holds a doctorate from the Sorbonne in France and has published various books. His book *Post-Zionism, Post-Holocaust: Three Essays on Denial, Forgetting, and the Delegitimation of Israel* sparked a major public debate in Israel when the original Hebrew version appeared in 2006.

"It seems as if Israel's main ideological adversaries outside the Arab and Muslim world are Israelis and Jews abroad. These people are much appreciated by Israel's non-Jewish enemies. The self-appointed Israeli true Left takes positions that are commonly referred to as post-Zionist. In fact, they are anti-Zionist.

"This ideology refuses to grant the Jewish people the right of self-determination and thus Israel's right to exist as a Jewish state. This means that it also denies that Israel can be both Jewish and democratic. Leading intellectuals, both Jewish and non-Jewish, play a major role in this new mutation of anti-Semitism."

Yakira: "There are no Holocaust deniers in Israel. Some Israeli academics and others of the radical Left, however, use the Holocaust as a major argument in undermining the moral justification of Israel and demonizing it. One should not underestimate the significance or the immorality of these positions.

"The discourse of the Israeli anti-Zionists is similar to that of parts of the Left and extreme Left abroad. In their discourse, anti-Zionists often employ the attitudes of philosopher Hannah Arendt toward Zionism. Although I doubt that if she were alive today, she would share their views. Arendt's book on Eichmann, in particular, has made her a symbol for the anti-Israeli sub-culture.

"With respect to the Holocaust's role in post-Zionism—in fact anti-Israelism—one finds certain analogies with Holocaust denial, namely with the claim that the Holocaust never occurred. This especially concerns deniers who come from the radical Left. This brand of denial, which is a peculiar phenomenon, is mainly French. What is special about it is not the Holocaust, which is its obsession, but more specifically, the existence of a Jewish state. Since, goes the claim, the Holocaust is the cause and only possible justification of Israel's existence, had it never happened, Israel's right to exist collapses.

"For the post-Zionists—actually anti-Zionists—too the Holocaust as such is not of interest. They posit falsely that the Holocaust is the universal and basic explanation for the existence of Israel and of its conduct. The structure of the argument of the two sides is the same.

"They develop further arguments based on the false premise that the Holocaust is the sole reason for the creation and existence of Israel. The international community, they claim, would never have supported Israel financially, politically, morally, militarily, if not for the extortion based on the Holocaust. The other side of this argument is that the Holocaust explains the Israeli psyche, ethos, politics of power, and its alleged violence.

"The truth is radically different. The foundations for the realization of the Zionist program were laid long before the Holocaust became even a possibility. Furthermore, the one instance in Jewish history where Jews had political power, but did not use it for killing, is in the Zionist movement. Israel fights its enemies, but with far more restraint than anyone else. The claim that the Israeli ethos is one of violence is libelous.

"The post-Zionists develop their false arguments in various directions. For instance they ask: 'Why should the Palestinians pay the price for what has been done to Jews in Europe?' This is also phrased as 'Israel is born in sin.' These demonizers then claim that in order to become better people, Israel and the Jews should forget about the Holocaust.

"Such arguments have gained certain presence in Israeli academia and in the Israeli cultural scene. Based on these, much literature has been disseminated and an intellectual community of similar-minded distorters created. The best way to advance internationally in academic circles is to be part of a system. One is then frequently invited abroad and gets published, even if one's work has no significant substance. In the last few years, we have witnessed the publication of a great number of post-Zionist books outside Israel.

"I have always belonged to the secular Left. Many Israelis who are part of the so-called Zionist Left, thought that their position was morally defensible. Some still barely realize that in the eyes of anti-Zionists, they belong with all other Israelis to a homogeneous criminal crowd. Many of them found out that they were opposing their own personal friends and colleagues.

"In the past we have only been apologetic about mistakes made by Israel, like anyone else. We have been far too timid in confronting our Israeli and Jewish enemies. We must now repeat consistently and loudly that anti-Zionism is an outrage and a sign of moral bankruptcy."

CAMERA: Fighting Distorted
Media Coverage of Israel

ANDREA LEVIN has been the executive director of the Boston-based Committee for Accuracy in Middle East Reporting in America (CAMERA) since 1990. This organization is both pioneer and leader in the field of pro-Israel media watching. Previously, Levin was associate editor of a public policy journal at Harvard's Kennedy School of Government.

"Pro-Israel media watching in the United States has grown rapidly over the past twenty years. The explosive expansion of the Internet enables media-monitoring organizations to transmit their findings quickly to many readers by email, or by publishing them on websites without incurring major expenses.

"Media coverage of the Middle East is often distorted. There are no enforceable codes of professional conduct which apply to the media. One can thus obtain change only in two ways. One is through private appeals for accuracy, balance, and fair play. The other is through public exposure of journalistic misconduct."

Levin says: "We follow all major print and electronic media in the United States as well as professional journals, websites, encyclopedias, travel guides, and so forth. Success in media watching is manifested in improved accuracy and context in the media criticized. Some of CAMERA's success

LIKE THE BBC.

a Columnist commentary

stories involve *The New York Times*, Reuters, and the Public Broadcasting Service (PBS).

"Our primary focus is on contacting the media and having them correct errors. This involves daily interactions between our professional staff and media outlets and also frequently involves CAMERA enlisting its activist network to challenge biased coverage. Beyond that, CAMERA's staff continuously post critiques on the CAMERA website and blog and write op-eds, letters, and articles that appear in newspapers, journals, and Internet sites, setting the record straight. In addition, we publish the *CAMERA Media Report* our flagship magazine, which is sent to journalists, CAMERA members, libraries, synagogues, and Congress.

"We've published monographs and special reports on, for instance, National Public Radio's bias, Arab building in Jerusalem, Jimmy Carter's biased apartheid book, the Gaza Cast Lead campaign, and the phenomenon of Jewish defamers of Israel. They are distributed to thousands of people, including elected officials. We also hold media conferences in many American cities and run full-page ads on key issues such as anti-Israel incitement and distorted coverage of terrorism. In the past, we've run ads about bias in *The Boston Globe*, *The Washington Post*, *The New York Times*, *The Los Angeles Times*, NPR, CNN, PBS, and more.

"CAMERA also has sixty-five thousand paying members, offices in six cities and thousands of active letter writers. We have regular contact with a great variety of experts when we need to check facts. We also have a program called CAMERA Fellows that offers intensive training for students in effective pro-Israeli activism.

"Of particular concern has been *The New York Times*, which continues to be influential, especially as a trendsetter for other media outlets that often echo its story choice and emphasis. As in the past, the newspaper is prone to placing the onus heavily on Israel for problems of the Palestinians and absence of peace. The role of the Palestinians in fueling conflict is slighted. In addition, *The New York Times* has been largely silent in the face of increasing global anti-Semitism, doing almost nothing to expose the biased enmity toward Israel. From the news pages to the opinion pages and even into the culture sections, *The New York Times* has an undeniable tilt against Israel. Many other mainstream media offer biased portrayals of Israel, such as *The New Yorker* magazine, *The Economist*, and *The Guardian*.

"The Internet has changed the dynamic, obviously, adding countless new voices to the discourse—some for the better and others for the worse.

"Countering distortions and improving information about Israel is a demanding process. Monitoring activities entail CAMERA staff members tracking the print and electronic media as thoroughly as possible and triaging that material to respond to the most important problems. Staff members contact editors and reporters in the field. The aim is to challenge all errors both in the news and the opinion pages and to get corrections on record.

"One way to measure success in this work is to monitor specific stories and issues that are covered inaccurately and when we've gotten them corrected on the record, to see whether the media outlet reports the same issue correctly in future coverage. Many times we've seen long-lasting impact and improved accuracy. Another aspect of success is the clear sense that after our intervention, there is more palpable caution in some newspapers and networks, greater attention to context, balance, and accuracy.

"The great challenge is the magnitude of coverage and on the Internet, the lack of standards and accountability. In 2007, CAMERA also launched a Spanish language project and in 2009, a Hebrew language website called Presspectiva, focused on educating Israeli readers about the importance of holding their own media accountable."

Levin concludes: "Getting the facts right is crucial. That is why correcting false statements is so important. Those corrections have an internal impact at the media outlet and often a lasting effect in changing coverage for the better."

HonestReporting:
Watching the International Media

S IMON PLOSKER is the managing editor of HonestReporting since
2005, having worked in public affairs for the Board of Deputies of
British Jews prior to immigrating to Israel in 2001. He holds degrees
from Birmingham University and the London School of Economics.

*"Israel should aim to ensure that it is fairly and accurately represented in the
international media. To do so, the media watch organization HonestReporting
monitors media, exposes cases of bias, and effects change through action and
education. This is very different from claiming that Israel is perfect. Many Israeli
citizens have issues with their own government on matters which are wrong and
they do not like. We do, however, want Israel to be held up to the same standards
as any other country."*

Plosker: "HonestReporting was founded in 2000 by a few students in London. They were incensed by the major anti-Israeli media bias in Britain at
the time of the renewed outbreak of Palestinian violence in 2000. This bias
continues until today. These students started sending out emails correcting
the false picture the media created. Their activities grew until a point where
they could no longer manage. With the initial help of the religious outreach
organization Aish Hatorah, HonestReporting—which now has charity

status in the United States and Israel—became fully independent in 2002.

"Our first major success came when *The New York Times* in 2000 reported that an Israeli policeman had beaten up a Palestinian on the Temple Mount. Later it became clear that the story was turned on its head. An American Jewish student, Tuvia Grossman, had been beaten up in an Arab neighborhood by a Palestinian mob. He was rescued by the Israeli policeman. The false version was reported by many media. The resulting campaign by HonestReporting forced *The New York Times* and other media to issue an apology and correction. A French district court in 2002 even instructed the daily *Liberation* and Associated Press to pay 4,500 euro each as damages to Grossman.

"A more recent example concerned CNN Senior Middle East Editor Octavia Nasr, who tweeted her admiration for and sadness at the passing of a spiritual guide of Hezbollah on her personal Twitter page. HonestReporting called for action and was cited as the major driver in exposing the affair, swiftly leading to Nasr's removal from her CNN post.

"HonestReporting is now a 'virtual' operation with the Internet as its main tool. Our main form of communication—apart from our website—is our email alerts. We try to cater to an audience which will not read lengthy research papers. People nowadays have very short attention spans. We supply them with sharp and short texts on which they can act. For those who want to know more, we provide links to material such as original newspaper articles, research organizations, or reliable blogs.

"Educating our readers to take action is very important, which is why we have also produced online advocacy lessons in the form of our Digital Diplomats videos as well as slide show presentations that can be used by activists in a practical way.

"Of course, encouraging letter writing to the media is an important part of our work and we like to reward the best in our 'Letter of the Month.' However, social media is increasingly becoming the new battleground of public opinion. We are at the forefront of using platforms such as Facebook and YouTube to promote our material and ensure that it is viewed way beyond the choir of core pro-Israel activists.

"An effective tool is the annual 'Dishonest Reporter Award.' The public can send their votes for our nominations of the worst examples of anti-Israeli bias. While the BBC is nearly always a contender for this negative honor, this year's award was won by *The Guardian*. We gave a long list of reasons why the paper stood out with skewed and sometimes vitriolic coverage of Israel. This included an 'anti-Semitic response to the Gilad Shalit swap.' They also published an op-ed by the Hamas Chief of International Relations Osama Hamdan, as well as a letter by the academic Ted Honderich, justifying Palestinian terror. These are only a few examples demonstrating the paper's obsessively negative treatment of Israel.

"Besides covering global English-language media as well as providing dedicated coverage of the UK media, HonestReporting has affiliates in Canada and Latin America. With over 150,000 subscribers and over 100,000 visits per month to our website, we hope to continue expanding to cover more European media outlets in the near future. The battle to defend Israel against media bias is unlikely to dissipate any time soon."

The BBC: Widespread Antipathy toward Israel

F ROM 2001–2006, TREVOR ASSERSON, a leading litigation lawyer, has undertaken six well-documented studies detailing the BBC's systematic bias against Israel. These may be found at www.bbcwatch.com. His methodology can also be used to analyze other media. He states: "The BBC's coverage of the Middle East is infected by an apparent widespread antipathy toward Israel. This distorted media reporting creates an atmosphere in which anti-Semitism can thrive. I felt the BBC should be analyzed because its significant influence on public opinion is combined with a unique obligation to produce 'impartial' news."

Asserson heads an Israeli law firm. Before coming to Israel, he was a senior international litigation partner in the London office of one of the world's largest law firms.

Asserson continues: "The BBC's monopoly derives from a legally binding contract with the British government. It has fifteen legal obligations under its charter, which include, among others: fairness, respect for truth, due accuracy, attachment to fundamental democratic principles, not broadcasting their own opinions on current affairs or public policy, ensuring that opposing views are not misrepresented, and not letting the audience gauge reporters' personal views.

"In my analysis I found that the BBC breached several of these guidelines, in some cases even most. Its news reports concerning Israel are distorted by omission, by inclusion, by only giving partial facts, by who is interviewed, and by the background information provided, or lack of it. I also found that there is a systemic problem with the BBC complaints system. The only way to establish all this factually was to do a proper forensic analysis. I then prepared my reports in the way in which a judge would expect the evidence to be presented in a court of law."

In a study "The BBC: The War on Iraq—An Analysis," which appeared in June 2003, Asserson and Lee Kern analyzed BBC coverage from 3–18 April 2003, when the war was a few days old until after the war had effectively ended. When comparing the BBC's treatment of the coalition forces in Iraq with its coverage of Israeli army operations, the authors found "that the partiality of the BBC's reporting quite possibly infects its coverage of all politically sensitive issues."

Asserson remarks: "In Iraq, Western coalition troops are described in warm and glowing terms, with sympathy being evoked for them both as individuals and for their military predicament. In contrast, Israeli troops are painted as faceless, ruthless, and brutal killers, with little or no understanding shown for their actions."

In his fourth BBC Watch's report in 2004, Asserson analyzed all documentaries on the subject of the Middle East shown on BBC 1 and 2 from late 2000 to June 2004. He found that the BBC was conducting "what amounts to something equivalent to a campaign to vilify Israel, broadcasting a documentary critical of Israel every two to three months . . . 88 percent of documentaries on the Israeli-Palestinian conflict paint either a negative impression of Israel or, in two cases, a positive image of Palestinians."

Asserson adds: "The thing that I did not include in my reports, which I probably should have, is the impressive record Israel has for protecting human rights. This evidence is entirely ignored by the BBC. Many examples can be given. For instance, the number of cases in which individual human rights are taken through the procedure of *order nisi* to Israel's Supreme Court and the way it protects individuals. Any democracy would be proud to have such a legal history of protection of individual rights. When one looks at the political context of daily violence against the civilian population in which these decisions are being made, it is even more remarkable.

"I do not think there has ever been a democratic country that can begin to compare with the decisions that the Israeli Supreme Court has made, under the pressures in which it finds itself. This is a completely positive area about Israel that is totally ignored by the BBC and many others.

"On the Palestinian side, matters that have been ignored include major issues such as Palestinian education, which is training people to hate. Another area is several Palestinian movements' aims to eradicate Israel. They are not concerned with territories. What Islamic Jihad and Hamas say is that it is their aim to destroy the whole of the State of Israel. In fact, the aim is to kill Jews wherever they are."

Asserson concludes: "On the basis of my interviews with present BBC journalists and those who have recently left, Israel is a hated state by many in the organization. What is insidious is that the BBC enjoys the hallmark of fair play and reasonableness because as an institution it is 'approved' by the British government. This cloak of fairness allows it to take a range of partial political stances in its broadcasting in an almost surreptitious way."

Exposing Anti-Semitism and Anti-Israelism through Documentaries

G LORIA GREENFIELD is founding president of Doc Emet Productions, where she focuses her work on Jewish identity, Jewish peoplehood, and the values of freedom and democracy.

"Doc Emet Productions wanted to build a documentary based upon Alan Dershowitz's bestselling book The Case for Israel, *which was published in 2003. We began working on* The Case for Israel: Democracy's Outpost *in 2006. At the time there was an unprecedented war of terror against Israel's civilian population, as well as an escalation of the demonization and delegitimization campaign against it.*

"The documentary presents a vigorous case for Israel. It demonstrates Israel's right to exist as the national homeland of the Jewish people, to protect its citizens from terrorism, and to defend its borders from hostile enemies. We felt that a movie would bring this detailed and penetrating analysis of the Arab-Israeli conflict to a broader audience."

Greenfield: "After the film was released in 2008, I began traveling extensively throughout North America engaging Jewish and non-Jewish audiences in post-screening discussions. I made several alarming observations: too many people mistakenly believed that the virulent hatred being expressed toward Israel related to policies and/or territory held by Israel. They falsely thought that the hatred was Israel's fault and if only Israel would make itself smaller and weaker, the hatred would dissipate.

"Many good and decent people were unaware of the resurgence of lethal anti-Semitism in regions around the world. Consequently, they were unable to see the hatred toward the Jewish state in context. Many were also unaware of the history of complicity of the Islamist movement with the Nazi regime during the Holocaust, as well as the Islamists' stated intent after the fall of the Nazi regime to continue Hitler's work.

"*The Case for Israel: Democracy's Outpost* was translated into Arabic, French, German, Hebrew, Japanese, Russian, and Spanish. It is still screening around the world in theaters, university and college campuses, parliaments, community centers, churches, and synagogues. It has been broadcast by the Israel Broadcasting Authority throughout the Middle East, by Telemadrid in Spain, and local stations in Latin America and the United States.

"Due to the reactions to the film, I realized one had to move away from the defensive stance of 'making the case' for Israel's right to exist. It was time to take an offensive position. An examination and exposé was needed of the lethal Jew hatred behind state-sanctioned calls to wipe Israel off the map and to murder Jews wherever they could be found.

"I then began a second documentary *Unmasked Judeophobia*. It opens with a statement by Elie Wiesel saying: 'Since 1945 I was not as afraid as I am now. I'm afraid because anti-Semitism that I thought belonged to the past, somehow survived. I was convinced in 1945 that anti-Semitism had died with its Jewish victims at Auschwitz and Treblinka, but I see, no, the Jews perished but anti-Semitism in some parts of the world is flourishing.' I felt this text set the appropriate tone for the film. Jew hatred is the plague of humanity, the cancerous disease that not only has the potential to murder all Jews, but also has the potential to destroy civilization.

"Unmasked Judeophobia was released on October 24, 2011, at the Paris Theater in New York City. Since then it has been screening throughout North America, South Africa, and Israel in similar venues as *The Case for Israel: Democracy's Outpost. Unmasked Judeophobia* has more recently begun to screen in the United Kingdom and Australia. It is currently being translated into Arabic, French, German, Hebrew, Italian, Portuguese, Russian, and Spanish and will begin its Latin American and European tour in the winter of 2012/13."

Greenfield remarks: "The film is dense and intense. It is not uncommon for the audience to feel both shaken awake, yet grateful for becoming more informed. Usually, the audience ends up asking for an action plan. Doc Emet Productions is now releasing *With Clarity and Courage: The Companion Activist Guide to Unmasked Judeophobia.* It is authored by Anna Kolodner and will be available for downloading at no charge at www.unmaskedthemovie.com.

"With Israeli audiences, there is a tendency to express frustration with the political leadership. The audience perceives insufficient governmental strategic thinking and action in response to the resurgence of lethal Jew hatred and the treatment of Israel as 'the Jew among the nations.'

"My next film project will examine the centrality of the land of Israel to Jewish identity along with the genesis of Zionism, the national liberation movement of the Jewish people. The roots of Zionism are *Lekh Le'kha,* God's calling to Abraham to leave his native land and his father's house for the land that God would show him."

Threats of Anti-Semitism and Terrorism on the Internet

Rabbi Abraham Cooper is associate dean of the Simon Wiesenthal Center in Los Angeles. For three and a half decades, Rabbi Cooper has overseen the SWC's international social action agenda, which ranges from worldwide anti-Semitism, Nazi war crimes and restitution, to extremist groups and tolerance education.

"The explosive rise in Internet usage in the present century has brought with it a new way of transmitting a wide range of classic anti-Semitic images and messages. Terrorist, racist, bigoted, and anti-Semitic sites have emerged in large numbers and are often linked to each other. Traditional hate groups such as neo-Nazis, the Ku Klux Klan, and skinheads proliferate on the net. Very different activist groups have built coalitions in the name of antiglobalization, anti-Americanism, and attacking Israel.

"In 1995, there was one hate site, Stormfront. It is still active and has hundreds of thousands of postings. The Simon Wiesenthal Center's Digital Terrorism and Hate Project, in its fourteenth year, currently monitors over fifteen thousand hate and terror-related sites. The exponential growth of viral social networking, however, makes the numbers game increasingly irrelevant, as a single posting, image, song, or YouTube video can reach untold thousands and beyond."

Cooper observes: "One can put up any website on the Internet, resurrect and dress up any idea, while targeting one's message to specific audiences. In this medium, one can even say that Jews drink the blood of their victims—and not be challenged or rebuked on the spot. Major anti-Semitic themes include September 11 mythology, Holocaust denial, blood libel, and *The Protocols of the Elders of Zion*. The Internet provides a powerful platform for well-known anti-Semitic themes, and forms part of a much larger online subculture of hate.

"A number of factors make the Internet attractive to hate promoters. It is cheap, difficult to monitor, and virtually impossible to keep a message off the Internet. Furthermore, it knows no borders; consequently, a minor player in a hate movement can now become a global operator.

"The cataclysmic threats from international terrorism have led to a major shift in how lawmakers and opinion makers in American society view the Internet. September 11 became a wake-up call in the United States. The main issue is no longer personal freedom of speech but rather basic communal safety. Regarding terrorism, there is a welcome trend away from being reactive to online threats, to becoming proactive. In the post-September 11 world, the authorities cannot afford to arrive after a terrorist event has taken place. To effectively stop terrorist acts, they must act before disaster strikes.

"Despite this welcome development, because of the First Amendment of the US Constitution, Americans are resistant to government interference in (mere) 'hate' speech. This helps to account for the fact that the United States is the offshore digital capital of hate. One example: Throughout the 1960s, 70s, 80s and 90s, Nazi books, which were illegal in Germany, were published there and then mailed throughout Germany. Websites forced off German servers have since appeared on American ones.

"To reduce the number and impact of hate sites, we must constantly engage online companies to do their share. When we deal with companies like Facebook, Google, and YouTube, we do our cause no favors by challenging the free-speech principle, but rather insist that the companies hold subscribers accountable when they violate the companies' own rules.

"There is a contractual agreement generated every time an online user presses the 'I agree' button. When you sign on for their service, you have to follow their rules. And their template online contracts give these companies the power to remove postings and even service. This approach yielded positive results and led to the deletion of many thousand websites, forums, and Facebook pages. At present, we give an imperfect Facebook a B+ for their cooperation in this arena. YouTube rates a D- and Twitter a Not Applicable. Twitter has yet to even acknowledge their service is regularly abused by terrorists."

Rabbi Cooper says Jewish groups must do much more to monitor the Internet because of the dangers involved. "As taxpayers in democracies, we have a right to ask the authorities to put part of that money into ensuring that terrorists do not destroy our democratic societies. When confronted with specific online threats from those supporting terrorism, we also have the right and obligation to seek protection from authorities. In addition, we must be vigilant and proactive to combat the political struggle against Zionism and Israel, and the growing campaigns to besmirch Judaism.

"We need a consortium approach to these challenges, which includes governments, law enforcements, intelligence agencies, NGOs, and the Internet community at large. Another big challenge remains to make educators, parents, and the media grasp the scope of danger that an uncontrolled Internet presents to the values of democracy. At the same time, online bigotry, anti-Semitism, and terrorism present ever-evolving threats to Israel and the Jewish people."

Fighting Discrimination
and Anti-Semitism on the Internet

R ONALD EISSENS is general director and cofounder of the Dutch NGO Magenta Foundation, which focuses on international human rights and antiracism. Along with Suzette Bronkhorst, he founded in the Netherlands the world's first complaint bureau for combating hatred on the Internet (MDI). He is also a cofounder of INACH.

"The International Network against Cyber Hate (INACH) fights discrimination and other forms of cyber hate on an international level by educating, acting for the removal of discriminatory postings, as well as initiating legal action. The network has twenty member organizations from nineteen countries. The Simon Wiesenthal Center Europe is also a member.

"There are major problems with Facebook concerning hate postings. The main problems involve postings about Holocaust denial. In a difficult conversation we had with the European director of Facebook he said: 'We remove most of the postings on Holocaust denial.' We said: 'You should remove all of them.' He replied: 'There is also Holocaust denial which is not considered hatred.' We laughed in his face and said: 'The essence of Holocaust denial is anti-Semitism.' Finally he said: 'I'm sorry, but these are my American boss Mr. Zuckerberg's views.'"

Eissens remarks: "On YouTube and Twitter, discriminatory remarks are also being posted. YouTube is unwilling to remove videos with discriminatory remarks, or does so only after much pressure and complaints. YouTube is now part of Google, and INACH is at present in discussions with the legal counsel of Google Europe, who has promised that our requests will be handled faster and better.

"The relationship with Twitter will hopefully also improve, as they will be opening regional offices in the near future. Until now, Twitter refused to remove discriminatory remarks because they are based in the United States and thus only have to comply with the lenient American legislation. The number of anti-Semitic postings and those about Holocaust denial on Twitter are fairly high.

"The Magenta subsidiary MDI follows discriminatory posts on the Internet in Dutch and acts against them. If we complain to an interactive website about a discriminatory post from a reader, it is often removed. In recent years, however, we also get many complaints about noninteractive websites where one cannot post reactions. The managers of these sites are often negative toward our demands for removal of discriminatory texts, because they have placed them there themselves. Partly because of this reason, our 'removal percentage' in 2011 has declined further to 71 percent. We have all in all made 516 demands for removal to managers. In 363 cases, their replies were positive."

Eissens clarifies: "MDI is not a monitoring organization. That would require much additional personnel, for which we do not have the funds. We are thus dependent upon those who contact us with complaints. This leads to 'underreporting' of discrimination on the Internet. Many people no longer complain because they believe the situation won't change. This is often the case with complaints about anti-Semitism related to hate postings about Israel.

"Until 2010, anti-Semitism, including Holocaust denial, was the main expression of discrimination on the Dutch language Internet. Gradually, discrimination against Muslims has passed it. Other groups facing discrimination are Eastern Europeans, homosexuals, Roma and Sinti, autochthonous Dutchmen, Antilleans, people from Surinam, Africans, Moroccans, and Turks. There is also discrimination on the basis of gender.

"We have to mark the difference between legally punishable postings and those which are discriminatory yet not illegal. The percentage of punishable postings on anti-Semitism is high. This is because most anti-Semitic postings are extreme and of a 'classic' nature. Regarding these there is a large Dutch jurisprudence.

"Anti-Semitism on the Internet is an insidious danger. It reintroduces old stereotypes, rehashes them, and allows them to permeate broad areas of the population. There are leading members in Dutch society who say: 'Look what is happening to the poor Palestinians. The Jews are acting like Nazis.' These people create the momentum for anti-Semitism in the Netherlands to develop further.

"Anti-Semitism on the Internet in the Dutch language is strongly developed in three major areas—North African websites, extreme Right-wing sites, and talkbacks on mainstream sites. The Dutch prosecution department of the Ministry of Justice is willing to prosecute expressions of anti-Semitism. If one writes: 'All Israelis in the Netherlands have to be killed,' the prosecution may also act because it is a call for violence in the Netherlands. But if one writes: 'All Israelis have to be killed,' or 'Ahmadinejad should launch a nuclear bomb on Tel Aviv so that all Israelis will be fried,' the prosecution office will do nothing.

"The reason is that Israelis are not Dutchmen and therefore anything can be written about them. This may be in breach of the International Convention on the Elimination of All Forms of Racial Discrimination of which the Netherlands is a signatory. However, the Dutch legal position is ambiguous on this issue and this enables prosecutors to ignore it."

Anti-Israeli Italians Abuse
Holocaust Memory

Angelo Pezzana is an Italian journalist. In 2001, he founded the website www.informazionecorretta.com. This site, which has many thousands of subscribers and viewers, has as its main purpose to provide on a daily basis a critical analysis of Italian media. It is also a leading source of information in Italy about political issues concerning Israel and anti-Semitism.

"In January 2012, Ricardo Pacifici, president of the Rome Jewish Community, said that every year around National Holocaust Memorial Day on January 27th: 'We witness outrages and provocations that we cannot tolerate anymore. We will respond in a decisive way.' Pacifici reacted after vandals had removed newly placed stumbling stone memorials. These are cobblestones with brass tops bearing the names of Holocaust victims. The stones are placed outside of buildings where those commemorated lived."

Pezzana says: "On July 20, 2000, the Italian Parliament voted in Law 211 with an explicit text: 'The Italian Republic recognizes the 27th of January —the date of the tearing down of the gates of Auschwitz—as Day of Remembrance for the race laws; the Italian persecution of Jewish citizens; the Italians who had been deported, imprisoned, or murdered; as well as those who in different organizations had opposed the extermination project and, at the risk of their own lives, saved other lives and protected the persecuted.'

"The law's text is clear. It is important that it also includes the responsibility of the Italian fascist collaborators. While the intentions of the Italian Parliament were good—to keep the memory alive—some results were negative, as Pacifici's statement indicates.

"The Shoah was already remembered publicly many years before this law was enacted, newspapers published testimonies of survivors, TV stations showed movies, and pertinent documentaries were prepared which contained original photographs from archives. In schools, texts from books of famous writers such as Primo Levi were read. Teachers discussed their content with their students. The authors were frequently invited to speak to the students.

"At that time, remembrance was still a respectful matter. Those who hated Israel did not dare to demonstrate this publicly toward those who had resurrected the Jewish state. These people even participated in the remembrance of murdered Jews, as they were afraid to be classified as anti-Semites.

"Marking the 27th of January as a day of remembrance has turned it into a national event where everyone can express his opinion, however miserable. The latter happens mostly in schools. Meetings are held with hundreds of students present where extreme leftist professors are invited to speak. They present the Shoah in a distorted way. This leads thereafter to a public debate usually linking the crimes of the Nazis to Israeli policies.

"These hate preachers are so verbally violent that moderates cannot state their opinions. I have participated in a number of these meetings. The horrific past was quickly forgotten in order to express hatred of Israel. The most recurrent sentence was: 'Israel is doing to the Palestinians what the Nazis did to the Jews.'

"These are not isolated events. They are the result of decades of propaganda which come out of the environments of left-wing politics, trade unions, and churches. This does not only concern the dominant Catholic Church, but also Protestants of various types. Churches very often host meetings with pro-Palestinian speakers. During these meetings, Israel is judged without being defended. Those attending these propaganda gatherings have no proper knowledge of the facts and are willing to accept whatever is stated. This the more so as priests are present who are in total agreement with whatever is being said.

"At higher intellectual venues like universities, for instance, anti-Israel Israelis are invited to speak. This is a dirty yet effective way to delegitimize Israel. Shlomo Sand, a history professor at Tel Aviv University, visited Italy in 2011. His book, *The Invention of the Jewish People*, has been translated into many languages. Sand claims that the Jewish people never existed. All this is part of the political war against Israel. It employs subtle techniques and thus seems even more convincing.

"Through these manipulations, the Shoah has become an effective tool against Israel. Using the excuse of the memory of six million murdered Jews, an effort is made to obtain the same results with respect to six million living Jews. The intention of the Italian Parliament was radically different, yet Law 211 is providing an unexpected platform for all those who seek in any way possible to defame the image of the State of Israel."

Israel: The Most Imperiled Member of Our Civilization

GIULIO MEOTTI is an Italian journalist and author. He holds a degree in Philosophy and is an editor at the daily *Il Foglio*. In 2010, he published *A New Shoah: The Untold Story of Israel's Victims of Terrorism*.

"Tiny Israel should matter greatly to the Western world, as it has become the most imperiled member of our civilization. The Jewish condition today is again the focal point of huge identity battles. Judaism is the source of humanity, law, morality, democracy, and thus, a beacon of hope for all. This is the most important single defining issue of our time. I wonder what will happen to other democracies if Israel goes under.

"The national rebirth in its original homeland of a people threatened with extinction for three thousand years should represent—especially in the eyes of Western civilization—a promise of redemption for all humanity. This is the more so since this people's arid and small country—on the borders between survival and destruction—is in the middle of a region that violently contests its right to exist. One does not have to be Jewish to understand that."

Meotti : "There were several reasons why I wrote *The New Shoah*. I believe in Western values and thus in the safety of the State of Israel. I am writing from Europe, a continent that is witnessing a major wave of monstrous new and radical anti-Semitism and the delegitimization of Israel's right to exist. This signals the risk of a major avalanche in Western society and perhaps even its fall. I also had a mission: rescuing Israeli victims from oblivion, giving them a name and a place by saving their stories.

"I spent six years tracking down Israeli witnesses to terrorist atrocities between 1994 and 2010, the so-called 'Oslo Wars.' I interviewed people who survived attacks as well as family members of victims who did not. I experienced very difficult moments and even thought about abandoning the project. It was a labor of six years of relentless determination, loneliness, and, perhaps, obsessive moral commitment.

"I did not write *A New Shoah* as an archival reminder, but rather as the reliving of a smaller-scale Shoah. This was not the genocide of millions of people killed merely because they were Jews living in Europe, but the murder of many individuals killed because they were Jews living in Israel. It is an immense black hole that in fifteen years has swallowed up 1,557 innocent men, women, and children and left more than 17,000 injured. I offer this book as a memorial chant for the martyred Jews which will transmit Israel's story to future generations. It is a rare document, and I hope one will read these stories repeatedly in the next decades toward the celebration of Israel's centennial anniversary.

"I knew I was going to pay a heavy price for publishing such a book. Nowadays to mention Israel in Italy in friendly tones, especially in journalistic and academic circles, is to risk facing a firestorm of condemnations or worse, personal attacks. I was called an 'agent of Israel,' 'a hard-core Zionist dumba,' 'despicable,' 'right-wing garbage,' 'Shylock,' and so on. A photo with my face and the Star of David impressed on it was published on Arab Internet sites. I received threatening emails like: 'Dear feces-eating insect, continue to scratch around the Zionist dung, the *hasbara* will give you thirty coins.' But I remain proud of the work I do. My son and this book are the main justifications of my existence.

"The daily *Il Foglio* which I write for has a small circulation, but all key people in Italian society read it. It is the only pro-Israel newspaper in Italy. During the Second Intifada in the worst months of 2002, Palestinian suicide murderers attacked Israeli hotels, shopping malls, restaurants, etc. They killed hundreds of innocent people. *Il Foglio* then called for a rally in Rome in favor of Israel. Thousands of people, many waving Israeli flags, gathered at sunset at Rome's City Hall atop the Capitoline Hill and made their way along the river Tiber to the main synagogue.

"Some held banners saying: 'We're With Israel.' Other marchers placed pebbles around the synagogue, a gesture recalling the Jewish custom of marking a grave. Israeli flags flew from windows in the neighborhood. *Il Foglio* made all this possible and fought a historic battle in favor of truth, justice, and the honor of the West, to which Israel belongs.

"In 2005, Iran's Mahmoud Ahmadinejad for the first time called to remove the State of Israel from the map. *Il Foglio's* editor, Giuliano Ferrara appealed for a public protest, saying that Italians should demonstrate 'to defend the right of Israel to exist.' This time the demonstration was in front of Iran's embassy in Rome. Politicians from the Left and Right took part. It was a wonderful night. Israel and the Jews knew that they were not alone."

The Middle East, Israel, Europe, and the Jews

AFSHIN ELLIAN is a well-known Dutch academic and intellectual. He was born in 1966 in Tehran, Iran. He came as a political refugee to the Netherlands in 1989. Ellian is professor of social cohesion, civics, and multiculturalism at Leiden University. Since the murder of Theo van Gogh in 2004, Dutch authorities provide him with bodyguards as his life is threatened due to his outspoken opinions about Islam.

"Unfortunately, Europe—including the Netherlands—is decadent. One can see this from the debate about the Palestinian-Israeli conflict. European TV stations choose to show selective pictures of Israeli actions against Palestinian terrorists. These pictures help Europe to forget its participation in the mass murder of the Jews. Thus, Europeans can forgive themselves for what they did in the Second World War.

"The clearest example of this was in April 2002, during Israeli military actions in Jenin. Palestinian fighters had settled in the middle of a refugee camp. They knowingly endangered their own civilians' lives. In the Netherlands, a false picture was created, as if three thousand Palestinians had been killed. When facts were checked, I was found right: fifty-three Palestinians were killed, most of whom were armed.

"This is not much if you compare it with what happens elsewhere in the world.

In Iran in 1988, between eight thousand and twelve thousand people were executed by the authorities. After an attack by the Mujahidin from Iraq, Ayatollah Khomeini asked how many of their adherents were in Iranian jails and why they weren't killed. A commission went from jail to jail and had people executed among which those who had not even been before a judge."

Ellian observes: "A number of native Dutchmen have confused a generation of non-Western immigrants. They told them: 'Remain Moroccan. Allah is a nice god and it is great that you eat couscous.' Nobody told them: 'It is good that you are a Dutchman now, learn to speak Dutch well, work hard, so that we can build a better future together.' This attitude will have to change.

"Similarly, discrimination and racism will have to be fought through a new national-civics offensive. My aim is not to convince Dutchmen that Moroccans are nice people. Not all of them are nice in any case. But it is important that they do find jobs.

"Often, I am scolded by radical youth who claim that I am an unpleasant person who wants a constitutional state. I once said: 'Away with multiculturalism.' We have a legal order which is based on two fundamentals—the Dutch Constitution and the Dutch language. The basic values on which our society is founded are part of that constitution. These include human rights, freedom of religion, and equal rights for men and women.

"These values should be advanced like the Americans promote them. I do not advocate chauvinism, racism, or nationalism, but constitutional patriotism. What makes the Netherlands more attractive than Morocco is the security of the law. Dutch policemen do not beat you up without reason.

"When the first generation of Moroccans came to the Netherlands, they did so because of economic possibilities and the security of the law. We now have problems with a number of young Moroccans who beat people up here. After the murder of Theo van Gogh by a Dutchman of Moroccan origin, the authorities felt a need to show that there were two extreme groups, radical Muslims and extreme Rightists.

"After this murder, however, it was mainly young children who were arrested for attempts of arson of mosques and Muslim schools. What they did was terrible, but we should not compare this to ideological international Muslim terrorism. The extreme Right has to be watched. If it becomes more important, it will have to be cut to size. Yet, we should not confuse its motivations with the radical ideology of many Muslims.

"For Dutch Jews, there is a double problem. Their tragedy is that they are attacked on two fronts—both by the extreme Right and by radical Muslims. The remainder of the Dutch population, however, does not suffer much from the extreme Right. One does not have to be a Jew to fight against anti-Semitism; it is a crime against humanity. We should also act against genocide, irrespective of who the targeted people are."

Ellian concludes: "Social peace in Europe is very tenuous, yet I do not think that there will be a new Hitler or Stalin. We could get chaos or even anarchy. People can start shooting at each other, maybe even in groups. Conflicts can get out of hand. That then, will lead to the 'Balkanization' of societies."

An American Observes
Anti-Israel Bias in France

N IDRA POLLER observes France through vignettes. She is an American who came to France in 1972 and has worked there since as a writer of fiction and translator from French to English. Ten years ago, she switched to journalism. Poller writes for various American publications, both hardcopy and online.

"My understanding of French media bias has changed over the past decade. I used to believe the press worked under a subtle form of government pressure, yet media hostility was rampant during the five-year term of the Sarkozy presidency and this included state-owned television networks.

"The left-wing, Third World-ist, anti-Zionist bias has spread throughout the free world. It is fueled by ill-concealed personal convictions of journalists and, with rare exceptions, their lack of integrity. Concerning French journalism, the sustained support for Charles Enderlin, twelve years after he produced the hoax that Palestinian youth Mohammed al-Dura was killed in front of the camera, allegedly by Israeli Defense Forces, is a significant indication of the dire consequences of unscrupulous journalism."

Poller: "Shocked by French reactions to the Second Intifada War against Israel which began in 2000 and the subsequent torrent of anti-Americanism after 9/11, I sought explanations in French culture and history. Having translated French texts into English for decades, I thought that the French language and its philosophical configuration shaped this perverse vision of current events. I saw the United States as a highly developed and powerful country and France as a declining nation, too cowardly to defend itself."

Regarding the French press, Poller says: "The French elite and media love Israelis and Jews who strongly criticize Israel. Some are hardly known in Israel, such as Michel Warshawski; others are more familiar like Ilan Pappe and Shlomo Sand. They are called upon to give their opinions as if they were speaking for mainstream Israelis. Then there are the Israeli stars: writers David Grossman, Amos Oz, and A. B. Yehoshua. They're the 'gold standard'—consulted like oracles at critical moments."

Poller says that a biased press uses many methods. "If Israel rushes humanitarian aid to an earthquake-stricken country, the media will either ignore it, downplay it, or find something negative to say about it. Grotesquely twisted narratives about the 'Israel-Palestinian' conflict are presented as documentaries. Doctored photos of alleged atrocities committed by Israeli soldiers or 'settlers' find their way onto front pages and prime-time news. Days later when the hoax is revealed, the media don't mention it."

Poller notes that the impact of all this comes slowly. "One could probably mobilize a larger, reasonably pro-Israel sector of public opinion if the French media were more diverse. Many people are ashamed to speak if they think that everybody disagrees with them and that it is bad to make their opinions heard.

"There is very little independent newsgathering internationally. Much of the foreign news comes from Agence France-Presse, a news agency that is partly owned by the French government and is biased against Israel. This has been repeatedly highlighted, pinpointed, analyzed, and denounced to no avail. It becomes possible due to an increasing fear in France of what the Muslims may do. The misreporting is not, however, limited to matters concerning Israel or Jews, but is global.

"There is little criticism of France in national media. It seems to be a deep-seated cultural problem. This is possibly connected to French education. French people constantly criticize their children, and this same attitude prevails in schools. Perhaps French people feel so threatened by signs of disapproval, because of the carping criticism they hear in their youth, that they reject it.

"The French societal system, however, shows multiple signs of breaking down. A significant number of teachers are physically abused by their students. Thugs shoot at the police. Courts often treat criminals like poor innocent victims. There is a shortage of jails.

"The violent climate in France affects the Jews as French citizens and, more dramatically, as Jews." Poller remarks that when speaking with French Jews, many admit that they do not see a future for Jews in the country. "Yet, as always in human history, people make individual decisions. They may say: 'I'll stay a bit longer,' or 'It's not really as bad as it looks and I'll stay,' or 'Our children will leave.'

"There is a clear trend among French Jews to move their children from public schools to private ones. Emigration to Israel is steady, but not massive. Lulled by a decrease in the number of anti-Semitic attacks, Jews are periodically stunned by horrific murders. Past victims were Sébastien Selam and Ilan Halimi. This year Mohammed Merah murdered Jews: Rabbi Jonathan Sandler, his sons Aryeh and Gavriel, and Miriam Monsonego. A three-fold increase in anti-Semitic attacks following this genocide-motivated murder brought the crisis close to a breaking point. French Jews are now demanding something more concrete than tearful ceremonies."

Sarkozy's Presidency, France, Jews, and Israel Today

FREDDY EYTAN is a journalist and former diplomat. He was Israel's ambassador to Mauritania and served in the embassies in Paris and Brussels. He is an expert on France's Middle East policy and has published twenty books. One of these, *Sarkozy, the Jewish World and Israel*, appeared in 2009 at the Alphée publishing house in Paris.

"Nicolas Sarkozy's attitude toward Israel during his presidency was very different from that of his predecessor, Chirac. He had inherited a past full of France's double play and disputes with Israel. Sarkozy broke with this approach. He made a clear distinction between bilateral French-Israeli relations and the problems of the Arab-Israeli conflict. In Sarkozy's approach, the development of France's relations with Israel was not a function of the progress of the peace process.

"Thus the strategic dialogue between the two countries intensified; France and Israel collaborated on major issues such as the combat against terrorism and the Iranian nuclear threat. Since Sarkozy became president in 2007, bilateral trade almost doubled to two billion euro in 2011. All this also made French Jews feel more comfortable."

Eytan: "Sarkozy's policy toward Israel derives from his background and worldview. On many occasions he mentioned proudly that his grandfather on his mother's side was Aaron Mallah, born as a Jew in Saloniki.

"Sarkozy's first visit to Yad Vashem shocked him. As the son of immigrants, he rose to become president of France he understood that the force of a nation resides in its memory. This was the more so in view of France's history during the German Occupation and its massive collaboration. Sarkozy thus proposed, during a dinner with the French umbrella organization CRIF, to intensify the study of the Shoah in the schools. He wanted to maintain the memory of each of the 11,400 French children deported to their death.

"Sarkozy is also a firm believer in French-American collaboration and reintegrated France in the NATO command. He reversed the decision of President Charles de Gaulle who wrongly thought that France could go it alone in its foreign policy. Sarkozy sees in Israel a fortress of the free world. He admires that it has developed a democratic society with great achievements in science, medicine, and technology. This is the more so as it thrives in the hostile and unstable environment of the Middle East.

"In 2009 during Israel's Cast Lead operation in Gaza, Sarkozy made two rapid visits to Jerusalem to see whether he could help end the fighting. Never before in the Fifth Republic had a President come to the Middle East during an armed conflict. Sarkozy had also visited Israel during the first Gulf War and donned a gas mask like the Israelis.

"Yet, like all other European leaders, Sarkozy thinks that Israel has to end its settlement policy and that the Palestinians should have a state with East Jerusalem as its capital. He was wrong in inviting two of the worst Arab dictators, Libya's Muammar Qaddafi and Syria's Bashir al Assad, to Paris. Though officially the president is in charge of foreign policy, the bad influence of the Foreign Ministry bureaucrats brought this off.

"Sarkozy hesitated whether to support Palestinian membership of UNESCO, which has its headquarters in Paris. He finally considered that Palestinian membership of a cultural organization was not such a problem.

Sarkozy was wrong on that as well. He has also compared the suffering of the Palestinians to that of the Jews, which is a falsification of history.

"As far as the combat against anti-Semitism is concerned, Sarkozy introduced a firm policy when he became minister of the interior in 2002. His predecessor, the Socialist Daniel Vaillant, had denied the existence of the problem which exploded in 2000. Sarkozy opposed the socialist policy of looking away when the perpetrators were descendants of North African immigrants rather than people from the extreme Right.

"When he became president, Sarkozy greatly increased the budget for security issues and continued the fight against anti-Semitism. He often said: 'Anti-Semitism cannot be explained, it has to be fought.' Sarkozy also remarked that insulting a Jew means insulting the French republic.

"Many Jews had a very positive view already of Sarkozy when he was mayor of Neuilly-sur-Seine, a suburb of Paris with a substantial Jewish population. That remained largely true during his presidency.

"His successor, the Socialist François Hollande, who was elected as president in June 2012, has had few contacts with the Jewish community. He has never visited Israel. The decision to investigate Arafat's death is negative for the peace process. It makes one think of the absurd honor France paid to Arafat's coffin. This failed Palestinian leader had also often been a guest of honor at then-president Chirac's palace.

"Presently, France has major economic problems. The Palestinian-Israeli conflict is low on Hollande's priority list. On the other hand, he will make major efforts to maintain good relations with Arab states. It is unlikely to bother him if that will be at Israel's expense."

Germany Bestows Awards upon Anti-Israel Inciters

B ENJAMIN WEINTHAL **is the European Affairs correspondent for** *The Jerusalem Post* **and a fellow of the Foundation for Defense of Democracies.**

"There is growing indifference in the Federal Republic toward Jew hatred and attacks on Israel. One of the many indicators of this is the awarding of prizes throughout the last decade by German organizations and politicians to Israel bashers, among them Jews. Some recipients have made statements which are within the definition of run-of-the-mill anti-Semitism.

"In the early 1980s, Austrian-born Erich Fried was the main anti-Zionist Jewish hero of the German Left. As a Jew, he became an 'insurance policy' to shield so-called 'Israel critics' from charges of anti-Semitism."

Weinthal says: "Fried was largely a lone wolf. Descriptions of a few more recent cases illustrate the present situation. Boris Palmer, the Green Party anti-Israel mayor of Tübingen, along with anti-Zionist Jew Evelyn Hecht-Galinski, coaxed the German government into awarding Felicia Langer the Federal Cross of Merit for her civil and humanitarian work. German President Horst Koehler presented it to her in 2009.

"Langer, an Israeli who became a German citizen, has toured Germany to bash Israel in front of high school audiences. She has compared Israeli military detention centers to concentration camps. Her promoting the equivalence of Israel with Nazi Germany helps alleviate German guilt over the Holocaust. Market demand for her 'services' is significant.

"Many German journalists, intellectuals, and politicians have anti-Israel leanings. They are checkmated by a climate in which the Holocaust still plays a role. These people have learned to do indirectly what they cannot accomplish directly. They shower hard-core anti-Israel Jews with prizes, feature stories, as well as interviews in major news outlets.

"Yet another example is German-born French Jewish intellectual Alfred Grosser. He has promoted reconciliation between Germans and the French. Frankfurt's then-Christian Democrat Mayor Petra Roth invited this Holocaust survivor to deliver the 2010 Kristallnacht speech in the Paul's Church. Grosser used his speech to draw parallels between the conduct of the Nazis and Israel. He is no Mideast expert, has no knowledge of Israel's history, nor any interest in Judaism. Grosser's passionately anti-Israel views have come to the fore in his recent body of writings. The Israeli Embassy protested him being chosen as speaker. Predictably, major media and the political class largely lined up behind Grosser. His speech became a combination of rewriting National Socialist Germany's history and attacking Israel's history.

"In his book *From Auschwitz to Jerusalem*, Grosser argued that Germany did not criticize Israel enough. Israel's Deputy Chief of Mission in Germany, Emmanuel Nahshon told me at the time that Frankfurt's decision to award Grosser the honor of speaking on November 9 'casts an unfortunate and unnecessary shadow on the event.' Nahshon called Grosser's criticism of Israel 'illegitimate and immoral' and his 'extreme opinions are tainted by self-hatred.'

"Roth would later help Judith Butler secure the Adorno Award in 2012. She is a Jewish anti-Israel professor of rhetoric at the University of Berkeley. Butler told a group of students in 2006 that Hamas and Hezbollah are 'progressive left-wing' organizations that belong to the global Left. She advocates the abolition of political Zionism.

"Controversial Lutheran Palestinian Reverend Mitri Raheb leads a small church in Bethlehem in the disputed territories. Former German President Roman Herzog decided in early 2012 to present Raheb with the German Media Prize. Herzog said that Raheb's 'acts are a symbol of humanity.'

"Israeli diplomats in Berlin told me at the time that Raheb is one of the authors of the Kairos document which calls for a boycott of Israel. It is a racist text that obstructs reconciliation between Palestinians and Israelis. They regretted that one of its authors received an award in Germany.

"Herzog ignored the protests of the Israeli Embassy, as well as those of German Christian and Jewish organizations. He also refused to answer press queries. This seems to be part and parcel of a trend to criticize Israel from a certain Christian perspective.

"Popular columnist Gunnar Schupelius of the Berlin *BZ* daily turned out to be a dissenter. This German Christian blasted Raheb's hostility to Jews. He based his column on a meeting with him in Bethlehem several years ago, when the pastor delivered a 'one-hour tirade against Israel.' Schupelius wrote that Raheb's 'wild look and tone could not be separated from his hate. His words were half-truths, or no truths at all.'

"Schupelius added that Raheb 'compared Israel's security wall between Israel and West Jordan with the Berlin Wall.' He did not mention that many children, women, and men were murdered in Israel before the wall was built. He also 'compared Israel with the racist state of South Africa during the time of apartheid.'

"One can add several other examples of German promotion of Israel-haters. When there are few counteracting forces to confront Germany's anti-Israel lobby, and swaths of the population oppose Israel's existence, this becomes a dangerous situation."

Belgian Socialists, Israel, and the Jews

JEHUDI KINAR was the Israeli ambassador to Belgium and Luxemburg from 2003 until the end of 2007. Before that, he had foreign postings in the Netherlands, Germany, the United States, and Canada.

"Belgium is a country with a complex political system that is difficult to analyze. It is a federal state and there are tensions between its two major populations, the Dutch-speaking Flemish and the French-speaking Walloons. Finally, 540 days after the last parliamentary elections, the Wallonian Socialist leader Elio Di Rupo was appointed prime minister of a broad six-party coalition. An analysis of his and his party's hostile attitude toward Israel for many years already, makes it easier to understand how he might conduct himself in future."

Kinar: "The Socialist Party (PS) is currently the dominant party in Wallonia. Di Rupo was a big disappointment for me, yet I should have known better. After he returned from Israel in 1999, when he was prime minister of the Walloon Region, Di Rupo said that he 'had not known that there are poor Jews.' During our first meeting I complained that while the Flemish Parliament maintained commercial and cultural treaties with Israel, similar agreements had been rejected by the Walloon and Brussels Parliaments. Wallonia had, however, such agreements with Libya and Cuba. Di Rupo answered that he would correct this after the elections; yet he did nothing.

"We had several other bad experiences with the Socialists. In 2001, a politically motivated court case was brought against Israeli Prime Minister Ariel Sharon and Israeli Generals Rafael Eitan and Amos Yaron regarding their alleged involvement in the murders of Palestinians by Christian militia in the Lebanese refugee camps Sabra and Shatila. We won in the district court. Then in 2003, the Wallonian and Flemish Socialists, the Greens, and the CDH—a Wallonian former Christian party—passed a rare retroactive change of law in the Senate which enabled prosecution of non-Belgian citizens for crimes committed elsewhere.

"After the kidnapping of Gilad Shalit in 2006, Di Rupo came out with a press release claiming Israel used this as a pretext to start a war against Lebanon. The Israeli Embassy responded by pointing out that the PS had never condemned rocket attacks from Gaza at the citizens of Sderot. Di Rupo later declared that he would continue his political line toward Israel 'despite the arrogant letter from the Israeli ambassador.' That letters from the Israeli ambassador did not deserve a response was a trademark of the PS.

"Another powerful figure in the party is Laurette Onkelinckx, then-deputy prime minister and justice minister. We met a number of times. She promised me she would speak with Di Rupo, as she could not believe that my letter had not been answered. Onkelinckx assumed there had been a technical glitch. When we did not receive an answer from Di Rupo, I sent her a letter. She did not acknowledge it. In the current government she is minister for social affairs and health and again deputy prime minister.

"Andre Flahaut, then-defense minister, was particularly problematic. He continues as chairman of the chamber. Flahaut was always available for meetings, yet came out with very strong anti-Israeli statements. In later years, he also took part in anti-Israeli demonstrations. Meetings with him were important because Belgium had soldiers in the United Nations Interim Force in Lebanon (UNIFIL). Like many politicians from various parties, Flahaut was surrounded by anti-Israeli advisers. Several had close advisers with Muslim backgrounds.

"A case apart is Philippe Moureaux, a former Belgian deputy prime minister and, until 2012, mayor of St.-Jans-Molenbeek. For years he asked the Israeli Embassy to provide Palestinian children from Bethlehem and Ramallah with exit visas so they could spend their vacations in Belgium. When I asked Moureaux why he did not organize a common visit for those children together with Jewish children from Sderot, he did not answer. A year later when he repeated his request, we asked the same question and got no reply. In June 2010, this not-so-young mayor (seventy-two) married Latifa Benaicha, who is of Muslim background.

"The most extreme anti-Israeli in the PS is Senator Pierre Galand. He has initiated many anti-Israeli motions in the Senate. He also heads various anti-Israel organizations such as the Belgian-Palestinian Association and the Lay Action Center. Galand was also secretary general of Oxfam Belgium during the period 1967–1996. Veronique De Keyser, a European PS parliamentarian, once declared that she wanted to strangle the Israeli ambassador. Many people thought she meant me. As she is a member of the European Parliament, I can clarify that she referred to my colleague who was the Israeli ambassador to the EU."

Kinar concludes: "Perhaps miracles do happen and the attitudes and manners of the Wallonian Socialists will improve now they head the government. Fortunately enough, some ministers from other coalition parties have a positive attitude toward Israel."

A Friend of Israel Exposes
Its Dutch Enemies

W IM KORTENOEVEN was a Dutch parliamentarian for the Freedom
Party from 2010 until 2012. He left the party in summer 2012
when its platform for the September parliamentary elections called for
the prohibition of all ritual slaughter. Before, Kortenoeven was in charge
of research and documentation at the Dutch pro-Israel lobby CIDI. He
grew up as an active Protestant, but later left the church.

*"At the United Nations, Iranian President Mahmoud Ahmadinejad once
predicted that the apocalyptic Mahdi will arrive, lead the war against the
Jews, and subjugate the entire world to Islam. This destruction is exactly what
Ahmadinejad and other Iranian leaders want to carry out. Religious fanatics
do not accept our rational arguments. I am concerned about my two sons, but
also about the future of the Netherlands and our culture. That is why I became
a parliamentarian.*

*"In 1993, I opposed the Oslo agreements explaining that they were a disastrous
trap. When Israeli Prime Minister Benjamin Netanyahu came to the Netherlands
in 2012, I said that Israel should construct as many settlements as possible in Judea
and Samaria. The country needs borders with strategic depth. In some areas, the
1967 armistice line is only twelve kilometers from the sea."*

Kortenoeven: "My 2007 book about Hamas was the first Dutch study on this organization. Despite its many terrorist acts, successive Dutch governments presented Hamas as a movement with different political, humanitarian, and military branches. The socioeconomic recruitment mechanism for the terror branch was seen as a hopeful alternative to the PLO. It would help build the desired Palestinian society.

"After the Netherlands changed its policy in 2003, it made a major effort to put Hamas on the European Union's list of terrorist organizations. This came about only after a few years. This development reflects the character and naïveté of Dutch Middle Eastern policy. Such mistakes can have fatal consequences—and not only for the Dutch. Yet once the Dutch become aware of their blunders, they often try to correct them. The question remains—if Europe had acknowledged Hamas' murderous intentions earlier, would there have been fewer murdered Israelis?

"My book received positive critiques from many scholars. However, not a single major Dutch paper reviewed it. The Jewish weekly *NIW* had it heavily critiqued by a member of a Jewish pro-Palestinian organization who saw Hamas as a reasonable alternative to the PLO. This, despite the fact that the Hamas charter and several spokesmen stress that all Jews have to be murdered and that Muslims will conquer the Western world. The book also documented the worldwide ambitions of the Muslim Brotherhood, of which Hamas is a supporter. Yet bearers of bad news, as my book was, aren't very welcome, and that is not only a Dutch phenomenon."

Kortenoeven continues: "In 1976 when I was 21, I came on my first visit to Israel. At a kibbutz on the Jordanian border, I worked on a former minefield with a tractor. This created a connection to the land for me. The link with Israel and its people has become central to my life. I also recognize the intrinsic value of the Jewish religion.

"My love for Israel led me to my previous position at CIDI. Israel has many opponents in the Netherlands. Several development aid organizations try to make Hamas acceptable. These Dutch 'humanitarian agitators' include Oxfam Novib, the Protestant ICCO and the Catholic Cordaid, as well as peace organizations such as the mainly Protestant IKV and the Catholic Pax Christi.

"Many Dutch media outlets have a negative influence on Israel's image. A number of factors are involved. One is sensationalism, another is Arab manipulation of the media vis-à-vis the openness of Israeli society. The change in character of the Dutch population also plays an increasing role. Political parties have a growing interest in the views of the Muslim minority, which now represents one million people among the sixteen million-plus general population.

"In the Labor Party, the situation is bad. A variety of its officials are Muslims. Since the Dutch municipal elections of 2006, Muslims are in control of various local branches. A number of these officials cannot even express themselves properly in the Dutch language. Some admitted publicly that they don't even know the party's platform.

"The extreme Left Socialist Party and the Green Left Party are even more dangerous for Israel. Many influential members see an ideological bond between international socialism and Islamism. They falsely believe that the so-called nonracist structure of Islam expresses international solidarity and justice. Furthermore, they view Muslims and other non-Western immigrants as a new proletariat and thus a target voter group.

"I often say in my lectures: 'It always starts with the Jews, but it never ends with them.' There are politicians in the Netherlands who also want to understand Israel's problems. They do not realize, however, that the clash of civilizations with Islam is unavoidable and borderless. The Netherlands will not be able to escape it in the long run."

Comparing Israeli Realities
with Dutch Ones

I N THE PAST DECADE, Ayaan Hirsi Ali became known worldwide as a nonfiction writer. In 2006, *Reader's Digest* gave her the European of the Year Award and said she best embodied Europe's contemporary values. Hirsi Ali was born in Somalia in 1969 and was granted asylum in the Netherlands in 1992. She left for the United States in spring 2006 after she had to resign from the Dutch Parliament because of a minister's ruling that she had never obtained Dutch nationality.

Hirsi Ali said she visited Israel a number of years ago, primarily to understand how it dealt so well with so many immigrants from different origins. "My main impression was that Israel is a liberal democracy. In the places I visited, including Jerusalem as well as Tel Aviv and its beaches, I saw that men and women are equal. One never knows what happens behind the scenes, but that is how it appears to the visitor. The many women in the army are also very visible."

Hirsi Ali: "I understood that a crucial element of success is the unifying factor among immigrants to Israel. Whether one arrives from Ethiopia or Russia, or one's grandparents immigrated from Europe, what binds them is being Jewish. Such a bond is lacking in the Netherlands. The background of the immigrants is diverse and also differs greatly from that of the Netherlands, including religion.

"I have visited the Palestinian quarters in Jerusalem as well. Their side is dilapidated, for which they blame the Israelis. In private, however, I met a young Palestinian who spoke excellent English. There were no cameras and no notebooks. He said the situation was partly their own fault, with much of the money sent from abroad to build Palestine being stolen by corrupt leaders.

"When I started to speak in the Netherlands about the corruption of the Palestinian Authority and the role of Arafat in the tragedy of Palestine, I did not get a large audience. Often one was talking to a wall. Many people reply that Israel first has to withdraw from the territories, and then all will be well with Palestine.

"Before I joined the Dutch Liberal Party, I was a member of the Labor Party. Their great model thinker is the Israeli philosopher Avishai Margalit, who promotes solidarity with those who are weak. In Socialist eyes, whoever isn't white or Western is a victim, and this includes Muslims, Palestinians, and immigrants. My position is that I am not a victim. I am responsible for my acts like anybody else and so are all people.

"I studied social work for a year in the Netherlands. Our teachers taught us to look with different eyes toward the immigrant and the foreigner. They thought racism was a phenomenon that only appears among whites. My family in Somalia, however, educated me as a racist and told me that we Muslims were very superior to the Christian Kenyans. My mother thinks they are half-monkeys.

"When I started to explain this truth in the class, the teacher responded that it was 'untrue and impossible.' I said: 'Yes, it is true.' I mentioned that I was living in the center for asylum seekers in the town of Ede and that the Somalis I knew there talked about native Dutchmen as uncircumcised, irreligious, and dirty.

"If a Dutchman says he doesn't want a Moroccan or a Turk as a neighbor, he is a racist. If a Moroccan says: 'I want to live next to other Moroccans,' that is viewed as a sign of group attachment, because he has been isolated by immigrating. So that is not considered racism. If a right-wing skinhead draws swastikas on a Jewish cemetery, that is Nazism and he will be punished. If a Moroccan immigrant does the same, it is an expression of his displeasure with the Israeli-Palestinian conflict.

"Defining an individual as an eternal victim is a fundamental mistake. Colored people, Muslims, and other non-Western immigrants are not victims. They are individuals who have come to the Netherlands in search of a better life. It is my responsibility to improve my life, and I am not asking the authorities to do it for me. I request only to live in an environment of peace and security. The Socialist worldview is different. Those who are not white and Christian, and do not share the ideas of Christian civilization, are victims by definition.

"Paradoxically enough, that attitude derives partly from the Holocaust, which created major guilt feelings in the Netherlands. Some people think the behavior of their countrymen toward the Jews during the war is something that should never be repeated. Thus they compensate by letting Muslims beat their wives and a few others beat up homosexuals or prepare to plant bombs. Such an attitude reflects mental illness."

Many Swedish Politicians against Israel

I LYA MEYER is vice-chair of the Sweden-Israel Friendship Asso- ciation, West Sweden branch. He is former chair of the Board of Information of the Gothenburg Jewish Community. He blogs at www.ilyameyer.com.

"There are no official calls by the Swedish government to discriminate against Israel. The current cabinet, a coalition of conservative, liberal, and centrist parties, formally adopts a neutral position in the Palestinian–Israeli conflict.

"This has to be qualified with insight into the distinct Swedish psyche. Swedes are often characterized by two traits: distaste for conflict and total dedication to an all-consuming need for consensus—irrespective of the principles or rights and wrongs of the case. In the Swedish mind-set, it is better to preserve consensus and adopt an inappropriate decision than to contradict the majority and insist on an appropriate one, even if this opposition is morally justified."

Meyer observes: "Another consideration must be added: Foreign Minister Carl Bildt, who belongs to the moderates (Conservatives), the coalition's largest party, has exhibited a consistent rabid anti-Israel position. He is widely regarded in Sweden as a political opportunist and seems to have international ambitions.

"Bildt often serves the interests of Arab and other Muslim countries. He may need their votes to be elected to an important position abroad. Bildt seems to be convinced that overt anti-Israelism will enhance his chances of personal advancement more than allegiance to principle. One example was his visit to Turkey after the illegal attempt by the Turkish vessel *Mavi Marmara* to break the Israel-imposed blockade of the Hamas enclave in Gaza in 2010.

"Bildt ensured he was photographed together with Swedish and Islamist militant activists. Analysts regarded it as rather incongruous for a moderate Swedish MP to rub shoulders with extreme leftists. They failed to factor in Bildt's ambitions and his animosity toward Israel.

"Another moderate politician of similar thinking is Gunilla Carlsson, minister for international development and cooperation. She claimed that 'Israel destroys EU-funded Palestinian infrastructure.' Carlsson avoids mentioning why Israel is put in the position of responding to repeated Arab attacks from that infrastructure. She makes no demands on Palestinians to stop using EU-funded infrastructure for staging attacks on Israel.

"Carlsson's approach appears to be that whatever the Arabs do, Israel's foremost obligation is to protect Palestinians from the consequences of their own criminal actions. Like many Swedes in leading political and media positions, she does not realize that denying that Palestinian Arabs can be responsible for their actions is inherently racist.

"Labor is Sweden's main left-wing opposition party. The others are the Green Party and the Communist Party—the latter recently rebranded the Left Party in a bid to boost its respectability. All three are vociferous in their constant criticism of the State of Israel. They are outspoken in their desire to officially recognize the State of Palestine should they come to power.

"Labor's gray eminence Pierre Schori was a protégé of the Israel-bashing Prime Minister Olof Palme. He consistently sings the praises of both Fidel Castro—calling him 'one of the greatest leaders in contemporary history'—

and Hamas Islamist leader Ismail Haniyeh. In 2009, Schori drew up a five-point plan which demanded punishing international sanctions against Israel. He did not propose any action whatsoever regarding Hamas for its role in firing thousands of missiles into civilian population centers in southern Israel.

"The left-wing opposition finds itself with the strangest of bedfellows: Moderate hardliners like Bildt, fanatic Islamists working to spread Sharia in Sweden, neo-Nazi groups that hate Jews and Muslims with equal fervor, and anarchist fringe groups. They all unite against Israel.

"In a league apart is Ilmar Reepalu, the populist Labor mayor of Sweden's third largest city, Malmö, where Muslim immigrants are a large minority. In 2009, a Davis Cup tennis match between Sweden and Israel was scheduled there. Reepalu tried to prohibit the match. When he failed, he issued a decree that no spectators should attend.

"Reepalu has made frequent anti-Semitic statements. This has prompted the Simon Wiesenthal Center to issue a travel warning advising Jews not to travel to Malmö for fear of being attacked. Moreover, President Obama's special envoy on anti-Semitism, Hannah Rosenthal, paid a visit to an unrepentant Reepalu to persuade him to abandon or at least moderate his stance.

"There is one political party in Parliament on which all the others have imposed a kind of unofficial boycott: the Sweden Democrats (SD). SD is against mass immigration, primarily from Muslim countries. It is also against circumcision, which impacts both Jews and Muslims. Despite its right-wing profile, SD is not noted for any other particular anti-Semitic or anti-Israel behavior."

Meyer concludes: "In the media, some churches, state-subsidized NGOs, and other parts of the Swedish cultural elite, there are many Israel bashers. Unfortunately, the politicized leadership of the Lutheran Church is particularly virulent in this respect. However, among government coalition parliamentarians, there are a number of Israel supporters. Without them, Swedish Jewry would be in dire straits."

Norway: Promoting Politically Correct Hatred of Israel

H ANNE NABINTU HERLAND is a Norwegian academic and a historian of religion. She has authored several successful books. The latest one, *Respect*, published in February 2012, received a lot of publicity and topped the country's best-seller list. Yet, there has been complete public silence regarding the sharp criticism she poses in the book against the current leftist government for its biased view on Israel.

"The current Labor/radical Left Norwegian government is promoting an extreme one-sided and negative stance toward Israel. It is responsible for creating a politically-correct hatred of Israel among many people in the country. This has made Norway, in my view, the most anti-Semitic country in the West. In Norwegian history, there has never been such an anti-Israeli attitude."

Herland says: "Control on public opinion is so strong in Norway that it is questionable whether it can be considered a free democratic state. The Labor Party has widely used the terror attack by Anders Breivik against it on July 22, 2011, to further discriminate against any opposition and shut down public debate."

She adds: "The Norwegian government indirectly accepts the Hamas agenda where its main goals include ethnic cleansing, terror, and genocide against the Jews. Labor Party's former Foreign Minister Jonas Gahr Støre regularly defends Hamas in newspapers abroad. In February 2011, he did this in the *International Herald Tribune*, for instance.

"In 2011, Støre was caught lying on a live program on Norwegian TV2. There he denied that he held continuous talks with Hamas leader Khaled Meshaal. Yet Støre had to admit this when the reporter told him that Meshaal had mentioned these conversations. What initially may have been an act of naïveté is by now suspect of deliberate malice. In the long term, Støre is tarnishing Norway's international reputation by acting as a Hamas defender.

"The way Norway funds Hamas with hundreds of millions of Norwegian kroner taxpayer's money is pure corruption. When African states buy their way to influence, we call it corruption. But in essence, the Labor Party is practicing the same—billions leave the country in order for Norway to buy friends in foreign states where they otherwise would have little or no influence.

"Despite major anti-Israel propaganda, a poll undertaken in 2011 by Norway's largest paper, *Verdens Gang*, found that 60 percent of the Norwegian people believe that Israel is right in claiming that coverage of it in Norwegian media is biased. This survey was done after the Israeli Embassy in Oslo had filed a complaint against the state broadcasting authority NRK for its biased reporting.

"This anti-Israelism is often accompanied by anti-Semitism. Jewish children in Norwegian schools particularly suffer from it. According to a study, many of them are harassed much more than other minorities.

"One may wonder why the Norwegian establishment is continuously badgering the only democracy in the Middle East. Many in Norway and Europe at large no longer recognize the historical link of their traditional culture with the Jewish people. Those who spread the Ten Commandments laid the infrastructure for civilized societies. The Jews have contributed greatly to the development of European culture."

In spring 2011, Herland published an article titled: "Norway is the most anti-Semitic country in the West." In it she wrote: "Culturally, we have much more in common with the Jewish people than one would think. Western civilization has its cradle in Greek and Roman contributions, but when it comes to values, in the Hebrew-Christian contribution.

. The European humanistic view of the dignity of human beings regardless of rank, class, or ethnicity, carries deep roots from Judaism. These values are at the core of what it means to belong to Western Civilization today."

Herland observes: "The new Western secular values imply a rejection of respect for our culture's historical link to the Jewish people. Many in the West do not understand that Islam's radical religious movement projects maximum resistance against what they perceive as Western decadence and domination.

"The new Muslim friends of many Western secularists treat several minorities in Islamic countries with violence. Sharia law is considered a cultural alternative to the Western legal system. What started as the Left's sympathy for the weak has turned into support for totalitarian coercion. This also includes backing a pronounced anti-Israelism. Today these undemocratic attitudes dominate the politically controlled voices in countries like Norway in a manner that clearly resembles Soviet propaganda.

"In March 2011, the renowned Harvard lawyer Alan Dershowitz came to Oslo. He offered to lecture at three Norwegian universities without payment. They all turned him down. Thereafter, Dershowitz wrote an article in *The Wall Street Journal* where he conveyed how anti-Semitic Norwegian academics let him know that he was *persona non grata*. This affair made me ashamed to be Norwegian. I am looking forward to the day when the present government will be defeated. Then hopefully, an end will come to their propaganda and the misleading image of Israel which they continuously portray to the Norwegian public."

Anti-Israelism in Finnish Politics

K EN SIKORSKI is a retired American living in Finland since 1987. He publishes on the internationally-known *Tundra Tabloids* blog. Without this publication, hardly anything regarding the anti-Israelism and anti-Semitism found in Finland would be known abroad.

"Nothing is known abroad about Finnish politics or the major incitement leveled against Israel by some of its politicians. One finds Israel's worst enemies in Finland's Parliament among the three left-wing parties. The Social Democrats have 42 parliamentarians and they are the second largest party in the 200-member Eduskunta (Parliament). The Left Alliance and the Green League have 14 and 10 seats, respectively.

"Social Democrat Minister of Foreign Affairs Erkki Tuomioja maintains a disingenuous air of impartiality and support for a 'two-state solution.' Yet in his previous term as foreign minister from 2000–2007, he compared Israel's behavior to that of the Nazis."

Sikorski elaborates: "In an interview in the magazine *Suomen Kuvalehti* in 2001, Tuomioja demonized the defensive measures Israel employed to counter Yasser Arafat's terrorist war by saying: 'It is quite shocking that some implement the same kind of policy toward the Palestinians which they themselves were victims of in the 1930s.'

"Before Tuomioja became foreign minister again in 2011, he signed an on-line petition of the Israeli Committee against House Demolitions (ICAHD) which opposed arms trade between Finland and Israel. Finnish arms sales to the Saudis, however, failed to elicit a negative response from him.

"In 2011, Tuomioja stated on a discussion panel that the existence of any country based on apartheid is not justified or stable. Afterwards, he tried to backpedal, yet already in 2003 he had described Israel's security fence using similar comparisons.

"Tuomioja's ministry oversees the Finnish funding of NGOs. In an NGO Monitor report from 2006, it was noted that 'Since 2000, the Palestinian-administered areas have been in the top sixteen recipients of Finnish development funds and have received roughly €28 million ($34m) in bilateral funds from Finland overall. . . . However, some of its funds are being diverted to promote politicized NGOs that contribute to incitement [against Israel].'

"Finland is one of the governments funding Palestinian school books. Ido Mizrachi from the Institute for Monitoring Peace and Cultural Tolerance in School Education (IMPACT-SE) said to the Knesset Education Committee in 2010 that 'official PA textbooks defined Jews as "snakes," "racists," "colonizers," and in addition they glorified "shahids."' In atlases in PA textbooks, Israel is not there," Sikorski added.

"The Left Alliance Party (Vasemmisto) is even worse. Its spokesman and current Minister of Culture Paavo Arhinmäki said in November 2011 on a local television program that Israel had participated in genocide of the Palestinians. A month earlier, the Ministry of Education sponsored an anti-Israel 'peace seminar.' The speakers included Israeli revisionist historian Illan Pappe and Electronic Intifada's Ali Abunima. A colleague of mine phoned the Ministry of Education to complain about the government office's involvement. He was informed that Arhinmäki's Ministry was responsible for the event.

"In a parliamentary debate about arms trade between Israel and Finland, a Left Alliance Party Parliamentarian Anna Kontula accused Israel of being a 'child torture state.' She stated that, in general, Finland shouldn't have anything to do with such a 'child torturing state.'

"The spokesman for the Left Alliance's youth division, Dan Koivulaakso, is a recurrent extreme voice in the anti-Israel movement. In 2010, several Finnish leftist activists were banned from entering Israel for ten years, after they had lied about their reasons for a visit. Koivulaakso then condemned both the Finnish Embassy for not sticking up for his comrades and Israel for not letting his lying party members in.

"One finds more of the same in the Green Party. In 2003, its Parliamentarian Anneli Sinnemäki chaired a panel on the Middle East conflict at the University of Helsinki. I recall that she mentioned her complete ignorance of the issues surrounding the conflict in the introduction of the seminar titled: 'Independence or Continued Occupation?' She thanked her colleagues on the panel for offering their 'expertise.' Its members all belonged to the hard Left.

"The Green Party's anti-Israel rhetoric often knows no bounds. Its former Chairman Osmo Soininvaara had at one time approved of a comment on his blog expressing the desire to see all Jews driven into the sea. Only after much outrage did he delete the comment without offering an apology.

"In 2009, the Green Party's online magazine, *Vihreä*, published an anti-Semitic cartoon where the Israeli flag was equated with the Nazi swastika emblem. According to the European Union Monitoring Centre on Racism and Xenophobia (EUMC), anti-Semitism includes comparing contemporary Israeli policy to that of the Nazis. The magazine never apologized for the cartoon, nor did any party politicians express any condemnation of it."

Sikorski concludes: "One finds major enemies of Israel in the Finnish Lutheran Church and among several NGO's as well. To analyze those, however, would require another full interview."

INTERVIEWS
DEMONIZING
THE JEWS

The Egyptian Beginning of Anti-Semitism's Millennia-Long History

PROFESSOR PIETER VAN DER HORST studied classical philology and literature. He has a PhD in theology. After completing his education, he was a professor of Jewish studies and other subjects at Utrecht University. Van der Horst is a member of the Royal Netherlands Academy of Arts and Sciences.

"As far as we know, Alexandria in Egypt was the birthplace of anti-Semitism's ideology. In Asia Minor, which is now Turkey, there were large Jewish communities as well from the fourth or third century BCE onward. However, there was no endemic hatred of the Jews as was the case in Alexandria.

"The initial indication of a negative attitude toward Jews is found at the beginning of the third century BCE in the writings of an Egyptian priest called Manetho. This Greek-speaking Egyptian devotes a large section of his main work, which deals with the history of Egypt, to the Exodus of the Israelites."

Van der Horst: "Manetho turns the story of the Exodus upside down. In the Bible it is an act of liberation of the Jewish people by God from Egyptian bondage. In Manetho's anti-biblical history, it is an expulsion of the Jews from Egypt at the command of the Egyptian gods, because their country had to be purified of unclean people.

"This 'anti-Jewish version of Exodus' sets the tone for a series of such retellings of the biblical story by subsequent writers in the second and first centuries BCE and later. Jew-hatred on a growing scale began after the conquest of the Middle East by Alexander the Great in the fourth century BCE. The exposure of one nation's culture to another is typical of the Hellenistic era, the period from Alexander onward. From then we see this kind of hatred gradually spreading more and more in Greek and later also in Roman society.

"The major first-century Jewish apologist Flavius Josephus dedicates a book—commonly known as *Contra Apionem, Against Apion*—to anti-Jewish slander in Greek and Egyptian-Greek literature of the preceding centuries. Josephus' text deals with, among other things, the climax of this literature by an Alexandrian Greek-speaking Egyptian named Apion who lived in the first half of the first century CE.

"Some of the earliest Greek observers of Judaism were positive. For instance two pupils of Aristotle, Theophrastus and Clearchus, made short and extremely favorable remarks about Jews. In philosophical circles, people sometimes expressed admiration for the Jews' rejection of a plurality of gods. That their single God was not even mentioned by name, nor pictured in whatever form, made them commendable to philosophical thinkers who tended to develop an abstract concept of a deity.

"Most anti-Jewish material from Greek and Latin authors is pre-Christian. There is no significant difference between Greek and Roman attitudes toward the Jews. When the Romans came into contact with Jews, they were also exposed to the anti-Jewish propaganda of several Greek authors. Although there is some anti-Jewish literature from outside Alexandria as well, it is significant that the main protagonists in the anti-Jewish propaganda came from that town; besides Manetho and Apion there are others. In Alexandria, the first anti-Jewish 'pogrom'—which we can define as an organized and officially tolerated attack on Jews—took place in the year 38 CE."

Van der Horst explains: "There is only one work referring to this pogrom. It is commonly called *In Flaccum* and was written by the Jewish philosopher Philo of Alexandria, who lived from about 25 BCE to 50 CE. He was a witness of the events. No one else makes mention of these dramatic incidents apart from Philo's somewhat later contemporary Flavius Josephus.

"The ancient hatred of the Jews derived in part from their being different, as far as the interhuman side of the matter is concerned. A second at least as important aspect is the negative views of Jewish monotheism. There was admiration for this monotheism in the more educated and philosophical circles, but elsewhere it evoked much anger because it was seen as a haughty exclusivism. Greeks and Romans regarded this denial of their truths as sheer arrogance. They did not feel themselves taken seriously as believers.

"One horrifying aspect of the history of Jew-hatred, namely, the twenty-three centuries of anti-Semitism which we know of, is the tenacity of so many motifs such as 'Jews are dangerous and enemies of humankind.' The image of the Jew as an enemy is grotesque and easily exposed as pure nonsense. Still, these images are kept alive among many millions of people all over the world. The fact that this is even possible is one of the most frightening aspects of the history of Jew-hatred."

The Deep Roots of
Protestant Anti-Semitism

PROFESSOR HANS JANSEN is the author of a major and frequently reprinted work in Dutch titled *Christian Theology after Auschwitz*. The subtitle of his first tome is *The History of 2000 Years of Church Anti-Semitism*. The second tome—in two volumes—is subtitled *The Roots of Anti-Semitism in the New Testament*. Jansen, a Dutch Protestant, taught history at the Flemish Free University in Brussels (1990–2000) and since 2002 teaches at the Simon Wiesenthal Institute in the same town.

"In many Jewish circles, there has been—for several decades—the false impression that Christian anti-Semitism was declining and would fade away over the course of a generation or two. This perception mainly stemmed from the major change in attitude toward the Jews by the Roman Catholic Church after the Holocaust.

"In the last decade, one has seen attacks and calls for boycotts against Israel by several mainstream Western Protestant denominations and the World Council of Churches. This raises new interest in the profound roots of Christian anti-Semitism and, in particular, its Protestant version."

Jansen observes: "Among the Protestants' founding fathers, Martin Luther was particularly anti-Semitic. No other important Catholic or Protestant theologian in history who wrote major works of exegesis, had as many horrible things to say about the Jews as Luther. In his latter days, he was a rabid anti-Semite.

"Initially, in 1523, Luther had written a book that was relatively positive toward Jews titled *Jesus Was a Born Jew.* Never before had a European theologian considered Jesus a Jew. This was major heresy. It was thus extraordinary to give a book such a title. He wrote this initial book with the intention that the Jews would convert to Christianity.

"Luther also wrote there that the Christian mission among the Jews had failed for so many centuries because the Roman Catholic Church had little to offer. He claimed that he was returning to the pure gospel of the New Testament and that the Catholic Church did not follow this. Luther wrongly thought that the Jews would accept this authentic gospel.

"By the time Luther wrote his main anti-Semitic book *About the Jews and Their Lies,* he was disappointed that the Jews had not yet converted. He now expressed himself in a way that would later be found in twentieth-century National Socialist texts and spiced his book with many defamatory remarks.

"Luther stated, for instance, that no people were as hungry for money as the Jews. If a Christian met a Jew, he should make the sign of the cross because a live devil was standing before him. Luther asserted that Jews dominated Christians. He recommended burning synagogues in honor of God and Christianity.

"Luther also wrote that Jewish homes must be broken down and destroyed. Jews should be housed in stalls and their books taken away. Furthermore, their rabbis must be prohibited from teaching on punishment of death. Jews should also not be allowed to take interest, nor should they move freely. The above passages are far from the worst that Luther wrote about Jews. He also accused them of wanting to kill Christians, executing ritual murders, and poisoning wells.

"Another reformer, Justus Jonas, translated Luther's anti-Jewish book into Latin. In the sixteenth century, one bookseller alone ordered as many as five thousand copies to fill orders from Italy and France.

"Luther's beliefs were abused by the Nazis. However anti-Semitic he was, Luther never preached that the Jews should be murdered. Julius Streicher considered Luther as his great master. Adolf Hitler and Joseph Goebbels also happily quoted from his works.

"In 1985, the World Federation of Lutherans distanced itself from Luther's anti-Semitic texts, claiming one had to understand them in the spirit of the time. His anti-Semitism largely remains a taboo subject for Lutherans. In my scholarly career, I have observed how difficult it is for people who have much admiration for Luther to be confronted with this aspect of him.

"To what extent do the reformers' anti-Jewish theology and Luther's legacy influence the present anti-Israeli attitudes of Protestant denominations? I think they play a role, but other influences are more important."

As far as the churches are concerned, Jansen concludes: "For two thousand years they have taught their followers to dislike Jews. It is mistaken to think this attitude can be overturned in a few decades. The new expressions of Christian hatred toward Israel reflect deep psychological processes. On the other hand, out of Christianity's positive tendencies toward Judaism, comes Christian and Evangelical support for Israel."

Muslim Conspiracy Theories Affect Jews

Professor Richard Landes of Boston University was trained as a Medievalist. He focuses on the interaction between elites and commoners in various societies. He has published many books and maintains several websites including The Second Draft and a blog, the *Augean Stables*.

"In this new century, we see a revival of conspiracy theories. Muslim societies are most prominent in the production, circulation, and belief in them. The best known conspiracy theory is probably that Americans themselves, or the Mossad, carried out the 9/11 terror attacks and not the jihadist Al-Qaeda perpetrators. This belief permeates the elites throughout the Muslim world. In quieter times, conspiracy theories remained on the fringe. After the Second World War, many people thought that Western culture had definitively marginalized them, including that 'warrant for genocide,' The Protocols of the Elders of Zion.

"Conspiracy theories coming out of the Muslim world are accompanied by another surprising phenomenon. In the past, conspiracists blamed a malevolent other—the Jews, the lepers, the witches, the communists. Now we find Western believers in conspiracy theories which target themselves—for instance on 9/11—in which they confirm the paranoid accusations of their enemies. Postmodern conspiracy theory's siren song runs: 'We' are to blame, 'our' enemy is innocent."

DEMONIZING ISRAEL AND THE JEWS

Landes observes: "In the last millennium of Western and Middle Eastern history, the more fevered the conspiracy theory, the more the Jews play a key role—from blood libels and international plots to global ambitions to enslave mankind. Communities terrified by their impotence in the face of the Black Death blamed the Jews, accusing them of poisoning the wells to kill their neighbors. Conspiracy theories simplify some people's moral universe: 'the bad things that happen to us are not our fault but due to the evil of others.'

"Conspiracy theories demand and justify extreme action. Anything is permitted when struggling for one's very existence against some agent plotting to destroy 'us.' At their worst, they are 'warrants for genocide.'

"The book *The Protocols of the Elders of Zion*, for example, is transparent forgery. Historians can document this for those readers who are impartial. But a rational approach has limited impact on believers who argue, as Hitler did, that even if *The Protocols* is forged, it represents a higher truth. The Shoah offers the most startling example: perpetrated by people in the grip of mass paranoia, who believed in a giant Jewish conspiracy.

"After the Second World War, Nazi conspiracy theories about the Jews were the beneficiaries of Arab hospitality. Faced with their humiliating failure to wipe out an independent state of *dhimmis* in the heart of Dar al-Islam, Arabs turned to *The Protocols*—not a ragtag army of Jews, but a vast international conspiracy defeated the might of seven Arab armies.

"Since 2000, however, the conspiracy mind-set has changed significantly in the Arab and Muslim world. The intensity, variety, and sophistication of the conspiracies' representations have risen exponentially. The mainstream media is host to all kinds of conspiracy narratives, from baked goods made by Jews with Muslim boys' blood, to elaborate film productions depicting horrendous, bloodthirsty Jewish conspiracies to destroy Arabs and Islam.

"The content of such outlets—from the Palestinian Authority TV to

Al Jazeera TV, to the major Egyptian daily *Al-Ahram*—reveals a degree of paranoia, hatemongering, and conspiracism with few parallels in history. In the Arab and Muslim world, conspiracy is publicly embraced by elites, including moderate, pro-Western, liberal Muslim circles. Conspiracy theory is so pervasive in this culture that, as one observer put it: 'In the Middle East, if you can't explain politics with a conspiracy theory, don't bother.' Future historians will probably find that present anti-Semitism in Arab and Muslim societies reached an even higher fever pitch than that of the Nazis.

"In the past, conspiracism inspired a certain fatalism among Muslims: who can fight so mighty an enemy? But in the twenty-first century, these narratives have spurred action. Indeed, they lie at the heart of the ideology behind suicide terror attacks, the bane of our new century.

"Many Western 'progressives' embrace these conspiracy theories which target them and the civic polities in which they live. This leads to the marriage of a premodern sadism and postmodern masochism. Muslims make paranoid accusations scapegoating the West. Hyper self-critical Westerners accept these as true.

"Organizations such as Hezbollah, Hamas, and Al-Qaeda shifted to the offensive at the beginning of the twenty-first century, *with* Western cooperation. In particular, they scapegoated Israel, the Jew among the nations. The first spectacular success occurred during the outbreak of the Second Intifada in the fall of 2000. The Palestinians may have lost on the field, but they won the propaganda war."

Landes concludes: "Any progressive or liberal who wants a vibrant multicultural, civic society in the twenty-first century, needs to confront the compulsive scapegoating of the Muslim world. We should say to them: 'Learning to live in peace with Israel is part of belonging to a mature global community. As long as you treat your own commoners as sacrificial victims on the altar of avenging your lost honor, do not complain to us about how "they" oppress "you."'"

Myths and Truth about Muslim
Anti-Semitism in Europe

D R. GÜNTHER JIKELI is an anti-Semitism researcher at the Kantor Center at Tel Aviv University and was awarded the Raul Wallenberg Prize. He earned his PhD at the Center for Research on Anti-Semitism in Berlin in 2011. From 2011 to 2012, he served as the OSCE/ODIHR (Office for Democratic Institutions and Human Rights) adviser on combating anti-Semitism. His book in German describes his research findings. Its title translates as, *Anti-Semitism and Observations on Discrimination among Young Muslims in Europe.*

Anti-Semitism among Muslim youngsters in Europe has specific characteristics which distinguish it from the hatred of Jews by people in surrounding societies. Yet it also has common elements. Many standard statements about the origins of Muslim anti-Semitism in Europe are without foundation. There is no proof that this hateful attitude is greatly influenced by the discrimination of Muslim youngsters in Western societies.

"I have conducted 117 interviews with Muslim youngsters of an average age of 19 in Berlin, Paris, and London. The majority voiced some or strong anti-Semitic feelings. They openly express their negative viewpoints toward Jews. This is often done with aggression and sometimes includes intentions to carry out anti-Semitic acts.

"Many youngsters I interviewed expressed 'classic' anti-Semitic stereotypes. Conspiracy theories and stereotypes which associate Jews with money are the most prominent. Jews are often deemed as rich and stingy. They are also frequently seen as being one entity with a common and evil Jewish interest. These archetypal stereotypes strengthen a negative and potentially threatening picture of 'The Jews' in the minds of these youngsters."

Jikeli says: "They usually do not differentiate at all between Jews and Israelis. Their view of the Middle East conflict can be used by them as a justification of a general, hostile attitude toward Jews including German, French, and English Jews. They often claim that Jews have stolen Palestinian-Arab, or alternatively, Muslim land. This is a major contention for them to delegitimize the State of Israel. The expression 'Jews kill children' is also heard frequently. It is a supportive argument for their opinion that Israel is fundamentally evil. As they do not make any distinction between Israelis and Jews in general, this becomes further proof for the 'vicious character' of Jews. It also makes them very emotive.

"The assumption of a general or even eternal enmity between Muslims (or Arabs) and Jews is widespread. This is often expressed in statements such as, 'Muslims and Jews are enemies,' or accordingly, 'Arabs dislike Jews.' This makes it difficult for youngsters who identify strongly as Muslims or Arabs to distance themselves from such views.

"We know that anti-Semitism is never rational. Yet some Muslim youngsters do not even try justifying their attitudes. For them, if someone is Jewish, that is sufficient reason for their loathing. From statements made by some interviewees, it emerges that negative attitudes toward Jews are the norm in their social environment. It is frightening that a number of them express a desire to attack Jews when they encounter them in their neighborhoods.

"Some discuss anti-Semitic acts carried out in their environment where the attackers have never been caught. Several interviewees approved of these aggressions. Awareness of the fact that others from their social, religious, and ethnic backgrounds attack Jews and remain uncaught and have not been clearly condemned enhances the normalization of violence against Jews in their circles."

Jikeli adds: "Differences between the interviewees of the three countries regarding their anti-Semitic viewpoints are surprisingly minor. One sees some divergence in their argumentation. German Muslims mention that Jews control the media and manipulate them in order to conceal Israel's 'atrocities.' In France, interviewees often say that Jews play a dominant role in the national TV media. In the UK this happens less, both in general and among Muslim interviewees.

"The word 'Jew' is used pejoratively in Germany and France by non-Muslims also. In the UK, this phenomenon is less known in general and among Muslim interviewees. Only in France are Jews often seen as 'exploiters.' Some Muslim youngsters mention that it is wrong that Jews allegedly have a better life in France than Muslims. It may well be that this stems from the fact that French Jews are often more visible than those in Germany and the UK and furthermore, that many French Jews are also immigrants from North Africa and that there is a certain feeling of competition.

"In Germany, some interviewees often use specific arguments they have picked up from society at large, such as the allegedly high Holocaust restitution payments made to Israel. Another argument frequently offered and believed is that Jews, in light of the Holocaust, 'should be better people than others, whereas Israel embodies the opposite.'

"Yet, there are also some Muslim youngsters who distance themselves from anti-Semitism. This happens even if they have been initially influenced by anti-Semitic views from their friends, family, and the media. This proves once again that people should not generalize."

Jikeli concludes: "Anti-Semitism may be strengthened further by referring to a general negative attitude by the Muslim community toward Jews. References to the Koran or the Hadith may also be used with the implication that Allah agrees with this viewpoint. Yet one should not falsely arrive at the common assumption that Muslim anti-Semitism is exclusively a product of hatred of Israel, or from Western 'classic' anti-Semitism, the teachings of Islam, or their Muslim identity. The reality is far more complex."

Anti-Semitism Embedded
in British Culture for a Thousand Years

P ROFESSOR ROBERT WISTRICH **holds the Neuberger Chair for Modern European and Jewish History at the Hebrew University of Jerusalem. Since 2002, he has been director of the Vidal Sassoon International Center for the Study of Anti-Semitism at that university.** *A Lethal Obsession*, **one of his recent books, discusses anti-Semitism from antiquity to the global jihad.**

"The anti-Zionist discourse in the UK probably exceeds that of most other Western societies. Anti-Semitism has achieved a degree of resonance, particularly in elite opinion, that makes the country a leader in encouraging discriminatory attitudes. The United Kingdom holds a pioneering position in promoting academic boycotts of Israel in Europe. The same is true for trade-union efforts at economic boycotts. Trotskyites who infiltrated the Labour Party and the trade unions back in the 1980s are an important factor in spreading this poison."

Wistrich adds: "There is also no other Western society where jihadi radicalism has proved as violent and dangerous as in the UK. Although anti-Semitism is not the determining factor in this extremism, it plays a role. This Islamist radicalism has helped shape the direction of overall anti-Semitism in the UK.

"Another pioneering role of the UK, especially in the area of anti-Israelism is the long-standing bias in BBC reporting and commentary about the Jewish world and Israel in particular. Double standards have long been a defining characteristic of its Middle East coverage. This has had debilitating consequences. The BBC plays a special role, owing to its long-established prestige as a news source widely considered to be objective. It carries a weight beyond that of any other Western media institution.

"Anti-Semitism in Great Britain has been around for almost a thousand years of recorded history. Medieval England already led in anti-Semitism. In the Middle Ages, England pioneered the blood libel. The Norwich case in 1144 marked the first time Jews were accused of using the blood of Christian children for the Passover unleavened bread (*matza*). In the twelfth century, medieval Britain was a persecutory Catholic society, particularly when it came to Jews. In this environment, the English Church was a leader in instituting cruel legislation and discriminatory conduct toward Jews, unparalleled in the rest of Europe.

"From the Norman Conquest of 1066 onward, there was a steady process—particularly during the thirteenth century—of persecution, forced conversion, extortion, and expropriation of Jews. This culminated in the expulsion of the Jews from England in 1290 under Edward I. It was the first ejection of a major Jewish community in Europe. Britain was not only the first country in medieval Europe to expel Jews, but also one of the last to take them back after more than 350 years.

"The long absence of Jews from the British Isles did not mean that in the intervening period anti-Semitism disappeared. This is an instructive early example of how society does not need the physical presence of Jews for the potency of the anti-Jewish stereotypes to penetrate the culture. The force of the anti-Jewish stereotype in classic English literature is so powerful that it ultimately is retained in the contemporary 'collective unconscious' of the country's culture.

"The 'Shylock' image influenced the entire West because it fits so well with the evolution of market capitalism from its early days. Shylock is the English archetype of the villainous Jew. Those who talk about how human-istic, universal, and empathetic his portrait is, are ignoring not only how it was perceived at the time, but its historical consequences.

"In Britain, as in much of Europe, the proclaimed antiracism of the left-wing variety often feeds the new anti-Semitism—which is primarily directed against Israel. If one suggests that such leftists are anti-Semites in disguise, they are likely to become enraged and retort that one is 'playing the anti-Semitic card.' This has become a code word for saying, as it were, 'You are a dishonest, deceitful, manipulative Jew,' or a 'lover of Jews.' Zion-ists supposedly use the 'accusation of anti-Semitism' to distort and silence the criticism of Israel and its human rights abuses. The word 'criticism' in this context is misplaced. It is a euphemism or license for the demonization of Israel. And that, in turn, is a major form of anti-Semitism in our time.

"Britain can pride itself, however, on the publication of the Report of the All-Party Inquiry into Anti-Semitism, which did a thorough—though not perfect—job of investigating the rise of anti-Jewish sentiment in the UK. The Report does not contradict anything I have been saying, though it was too soft on Muslim anti-Semitism."

Sixty Years of French Intellectual Bias against Israel

S IMON EPSTEIN **teaches at Hebrew University in Jerusalem. He is a former director of its Vidal Sassoon International Center for the Study of Anti-Semitism. Since 1982, Epstein has published various books and articles on anti-Semitism and racism.**

"In the present century, France has stood out in a negative light, not only because of the many violent assaults on Jews and their institutions, but also due to the frequent anti-Semitic intellectual and media attacks on Israel. The origins of French intellectual anti-Israelism date back almost to the creation of the Jewish state. To gain a perspective on present problems, one must have a better understanding of the historical development and nature of French intellectualism."

Epstein: "In November 1947, the Soviet Union voted at the United Nations for the creation of the Jewish state. Therefore, French communist intellectuals initially had a positive attitude toward Israel. When after a few years the Soviet Union started to adopt anti-Zionist and anti-Semitic positions, the views of many French communists also shifted.

"In January 1953, the daily *Pravda* broke the news of the indictment of nine doctors, six of whom were Jews. They were accused of having caused the death of leading Soviet figures by incorrect diagnoses and treatment and of planning further 'assassinations.' At the same time, the Soviet press intensified its campaign against 'Cosmopolitanism and Zionism.'

"French communist intellectuals organized a major solidarity rally in Paris in support of the official Soviet position on the 'doctors plot.' The organizers saw to it that there were enough Jews among the many speakers on the podium.

"The message of the speakers was frightening. Many of them explained that it was normal to suspect doctors of poisoning people—one only had to look at Mengele's role in Auschwitz. If he was capable of what he did, why should other physicians not use poison? A Jewish physician was among those who publicly took this stand. As a medical doctor, he bore witness that the charge was not absurd. He also based his position on the misconduct of German physicians during the Second World War, stating that it could not be definitely excluded that Jews or Zionists decided to poison Soviet personalities. In later years however, he greatly regretted his words. The Russian physicians have since been rehabilitated.

"The moral aberration of these 'witnesses' was so great because France, unlike the Soviet Union, was a free country. The speakers spoke voluntarily. Communist organizations also arranged a large media campaign. Intellectuals wrote articles about the 'criminal doctors,' or signed petitions against them. Again, Communist organizers saw to it that many Jews were among the signatories.

"Within the party there were Jewish organizations which were mobilized for protests on the 'doctors plot.' Many anti-Semitic themes used then resurfaced in anti-Israel campaigns following the Six-Day War in 1967.

"The initial intensity of these campaigns was much lower than in the prewar decade. Anti-Zionist publicity was almost entirely fed by Communists. They however always recognized—like the Soviet Union—Israel's right to exist. In the 1950s, Communists dominated the French Left.

Trotskyism was insignificant, expanding only twenty years later after the events of May 1968, when Communism began losing power."

Epstein explains: "The fascination Marxism exuded onto major parts of the French Left led to a much larger percentage of intellectuals being attracted to it than elsewhere in the West, with the possible exception of Italy. The multiple deviations of French intellectualism derive from its general characteristics, i.e., a tendency toward extremism. The French intellectual's position is by necessity one of representing absolute morality and imparting the feeling that his analysis is the only justified one. He must be confrontational and define enemies; nuances and intermediary positions are not permitted.

"Another characteristic concerns the way the intellectual expresses himself. Language, which is very important, must always be complex and contain highly rhetorical aspects. Thought departs from reality and is embodied in theoretical constructions aspiring to an absolute world. The combination of these features stimulates major intellectual distortions.

"Since the 1970s, many French thinkers have been interested in the role of words and the multiplicity of concepts. They have generated schools of intellectuals whose words are incomprehensible. When standing before an audience, they produce endless abstractions without using simple words. This leads to an absurd intellectualism, which also exists in the social sciences elsewhere but was initially developed in France.

"In the current century, the intellectual anti-Semitic outburst greatly increased in intensity. An initial deafening silence surrounding the violent anti-Semitic incidents in the first years was accompanied by a stream of verbal attacks on Israel which rehash arguments from earlier anti-Zionist campaigns. Moderate intellectuals compared Sharon to Milosevic; extremists compared him to Hitler. Nowadays when people still comment on 'the new anti-Semitism,' I wonder whether they are unaware of these many decades of history."

Contemporary French Anti-Semitism: A Barometer for Gauging Problems in Society

SHMUEL TRIGANO **is professor of sociology at Paris University, president of the Observatoire du Monde Juif, and author of numerous books focusing on Jewish philosophy and Jewish political thought.**

"The possibility of the renascence of an anti-Semitic (anti-Zionist) current in French opinion merging with a classical Islamic anti-Judaism, mirrors the situation of French society. Newcomers, as well as citizens, showed how—for a decade now—to instrumentalize the symbolic and mythological position of Jews in French society and European mentality in order to advance their own agenda. Several different political parties, politicians, and publicists also used Jews as a tool in various domains.

"There was a major anti-Semitic wave in French public opinion when the second Palestinian uprising broke out in 2000. Israel was painted as monstrous, a Nazi state intent on killing children. This anti-Israeli discourse has deeper roots. Anti-Semitic stereotypes were already present—albeit in the background—during the Oslo process. Jews were then often accused of having 'memorialized the Shoah too much,' to exploit it for prestige, power, and appropriation."

Trigano remarked that in order to understand the current situation, it is essential to remember not only how the major increase in violent anti-Semitism in France started in 2000, but also the public's reaction to it. "It was, as far as the postwar period is concerned, unprecedented. Its main perpetrators were French citizens from Muslim Arab and sub-Saharan African immigrant backgrounds. There had been similar incidents—although not as many—during the first Gulf War at the beginning of the 1990s."

Trigano recalled that anti-Semitic violence went largely unreported by both the press and public authorities for several months. "Even Jewish organizations remained silent, most probably at the request of the Socialist-led government of Prime Minister Lionel Jospin as we discovered later. This silence was another factor why the Jewish community felt abandoned by both the French authorities and complacent society.

"The situation of the Jews in France was aggravated as various media expressed opinions claiming that the violence and hate was quite understandable in view of events in the Middle East and Israel's policies. This implied that the destiny of French Jews was determined by Israeli policies and French criticism of it.

"During the first months of attacks, French Jewry requested help, but no one listened. This led many French Jews to realize that their place and citizenship in the country was now questionable. They understood that the authorities were willing to sacrifice the Jewish community to maintain social peace. This attitude was reinforced by the French pro-Arab policy in the Iraq War.

"Jewish citizens could not understand that violent acts were being committed against them in the name of developments 3,000 kilometers away. Today, there are those who still remember the words of Hubert Védrine, former Socialist minister of foreign affairs, which have been repeated in different variations by several politicians: 'One does not necessarily have to be shocked that young Frenchmen of immigrant origin have compassion for the Palestinians and are very agitated because of what is happening to them.'"

Trigano remarked: "Individual Jews reacted according to experiences from the past. A well-known French Jewish psychoanalyst, the late Janine Chasseguet-Smirgel, told me that for her it recalled the 1930s. It seemed to me initially an exaggeration, because France is supposed to be a democratic and open society. Yet it was difficult to understand how the discourse of a liberal state's free press could uniformly follow the government. Thereafter I understood the Soviet Union's reality better.

"My own associations were with our family's flight from Algeria in June 1962, when we waited for two days in a military airport with only two suitcases. We had closed the door of our home and left, as the public authorities had abandoned us. We had to save ourselves in order not to be killed in the chaos.

"These traumatic feelings have not left French Jews, even though two years later, Nicolas Sarkozy as Minister of the Interior made an attempt to combat anti-Semitism. Perhaps public awareness of the problem came too late. In France, self-censorship concerning anti-Semitic discourse has broken down. One finds frequent anti-Semitic expressions in the public domain. A democratic government cannot change this phenomenon in any way. The media and the government falsely call anti-Semitism 'inter-ethnic tensions.'

"One consequence of hostility directed at Jews is the increasing development of a Jewish mental and behavioral ghetto. They feel marginalized and subsequently withdrew from broader society to be among Jewish friends. Another phenomenon in the new century is the increasing number of students and teachers in private Jewish schools because they feel vulnerable and defenseless in public schools.

"The ideological process of promoting anti-Jewish hatred, however, has continued for more than ten years against a background where Islamists, extreme left- and right-wing circles meet. Jews are too feeble an electorate to expect change from any political current. Generally speaking, there is little sympathy for the Jews and Israel in French public opinion."

Muslim Anti-Semitism in France

S INCE 2007, DR. RICHARD PRASQUIER has been chairman of CRIF, the umbrella of French Jewish organizations. He is a cardiologist by profession.

"Since the beginning of this century, Muslim anti-Semitism has become the most extreme form of Jew-hatred in France. The murder of a Jewish teacher and three children at the Otzar HaTorah School in Toulouse in March 2012 underlined this. The murderer, Mohammed Merah, claimed that he acted out of solidarity with the Palestinians. He also killed three French soldiers out of his hatred for France.

"Merah's elder brother Abdelghani told me that his mother imbued all of her children with strong anti-Semitic sentiments. He repeats this claim in a book he published. His sister stated how proud she is of her brother Mohammed on French television. When previous President Nicolas Sarkozy proposed a minute of silence in schools for the victims, Muslim students in some schools were unwilling to comply."

Prasquier says: "We told the leaders from representative Muslim bodies that they should condemn the Merah murders. They did condemn them, but mainly to try to prove that Muslims were also victims of Mohammed Merah, because his deeds had fueled Islamophobia. Most official Muslim organizations are weak and enjoy scant support in the Muslim community. Radicals have succeeded in silencing many of the Muslim moderates. We also see an increasing influence coming from Arab countries among French Muslims. This is in particularly true for Qatar, which is also influential in French sports. There is, however, some good news. Eighteen French imams traveled in 2012 to Israel. Their willingness to visit was a courageous act, since many of them were subjected to major criticism from other Muslims.

"The Merah murders had different effects in France. Some media are beginning to understand that radical Muslims endanger the republican ideals which embody the essence of French values. In an op-ed in *Le Monde*, I explained how radical Islam shares common traits with Nazism.

"Anti-Semitism in France has traditionally been identified as coming from the extreme Right. This is true, but it is declining. There is also significant anti-Semitism among the left-wing. This mainly expresses itself as anti-Zionism. One may oppose the Zionist idea, yet if people single out Zionism amongst ideologies, they thus become anti-Semites.

"Leftist anti-Semitism has ancient roots. In the nineteenth century, there was strong anti-Semitism among precursors of socialism. Nowadays, left-wing anti-Semites falsely compare the Israeli attitude to the Palestinians to that of France in its former colonies. They see Palestinians as victims of a nonexistent Israeli 'colonialism' and project their own guilt feelings upon Israelis.

"The situation is even worse as most French media are anti-Israel. CRIF invited in 2012 a group of 66 candidate journalists to Israel. They came from the country's most prestigious journalist school in Lille. We know from internal surveys that they overwhelmingly voted against Nicolas Sarkozy in the recent presidential election and that a significant number of them supported rather extreme left-wing candidates.

"French anti-Semitism is a complex phenomenon. Not long before the elections, the leading Socialist candidate was Dominique Strauss-Kahn, who identifies publicly as Jewish. His Judaism only became an issue on some extreme right-wing blogs. Sarkozy, however, was convinced that much of the opposition against himself was due to anti-Semitism, as he was falsely perceived as being Jewish because his maternal grandfather was of Jewish origin.

"Before he became president, François Hollande did not have many relations with Jewish organizations. He, though, was always considered strongly opposed to anti-Semitism. Since his election, Hollande has made it a point to show strong support for French Jewry. He expressed this at an annual memorial ceremony for deported Jews in Paris in July 2012 and did so once again at the inauguration of a memorial center at Drancy in September. Most arrested French Jews were deported to their death from this transit camp. Hollande also accompanied Benjamin Netanyahu to Toulouse and stated that the Israeli prime minister was justified in showing interest in French anti-Semitism.

"Socialist Minister of the Interior Manuel Valls has also come out strongly against anti-Semitism. Many Socialists now in power have sympathy for Israel. This is, however, much less the case with the new generation."

Prasquier concludes: "On one hand, French Jewry is concerned about its own future. There is some Jewish emigration taking place, of which only a minority is leaving for Israel. On the other hand, we remain a major Jewish community by international standards. There are signs of hope as more Frenchmen recognize the dangers coming out of radical Muslim circles. Jews should not accept unhealthy alliances with the populist extreme Right, which tries to cater to them on the basis of a common fear of Islamism. It must be emphasized that French Jewry acts because of the danger radical Muslims pose to the republican character of France. One should not stress that its main motives are the dangers radical Muslims pose specifically to Jews."

Netherlands: Both Anti-Semitism and Sympathy for Jews on the Rise

CHIEF RABBI BINYOMIN JACOBS is head of the IPOR—the rabbinate for the Jewish communities outside of Amsterdam, The Hague, and Rotterdam—and also the rabbi of the Sinai Center, the only Jewish psychiatric hospital in Europe.

"People often insult me in public. It can happen almost anywhere, such as at the train station in Rotterdam or in the center of Amersfoort, the town where I live. For instance, someone may shout at me 'Yehoud'—a negative term for a Jew in Arabic. When I walked home from our synagogue a few years ago, a child of about ten years old shouted out 'Dirty, stinking Jew.'

"At train stations where a lot of youngsters hang out, I am almost always insulted. These shouts do not only come from non-Western immigrants, but from native Dutchmen as well. If I go to the synagogue on Saturday afternoon, I am shouted at not only at the mosque but also near the hockeyfield."

Jacobs says: "I perceive that the aggression against Jews who are recognizable by their dress has increased greatly. On the other hand, there is also an increase in sympathy toward us. When I enter a train, someone may just shake my hand and say 'Shalom' or something positive about Jews and Israel.

"Developments in the Netherlands are worrisome. Whenever something dramatic happens in Israel, people start shouting at you 'Israel' or 'Hamas, Hamas, Jews to the Gas.' Once I had a very shocking experience. A non-Jewish psychologist and I entered a train full of Feyenoord soccer fans. They started to chant: 'Jews to the gas.' I had the feeling that this whole train of 'ordinary Dutchmen' was against us.

"The psychologist shrank from fear. I thought that displaying signs of anxiety wouldn't be helpful, thus I feigned that I was indifferent to it, as a sign of strength. One may consider this incident as just an act of hooliganism, yet if one of these idiots had attacked us, many more would have probably followed him.

"Across from our house is a school with children who come from greatly varied backgrounds. One day a Turkish lady walked up to me, holding a young child tightly by the hand. The child looked deadly afraid. The lady said to the child: 'Don't be frightened. This grandfather won't hurt you. He's a nice man.' The boy seemed to be of Moroccan origin and thought that I would kidnap him. He had apparently been told that Jews are dangerous. That lady wanted to teach him otherwise.

"Such feelings are heightened because in the mosques here, a film was shown in which Israel is falsely accused of kidnapping Arab children to give their eyes to Jewish children. Afterwards, the Arab child is blind and the Jewish child can see again. A kid who has heard this is obviously afraid.

"At a kindergarten, a three-year-old child from Somalia called me 'a dirty Jew.' I cannot debate with a small child! The teacher who was Dutch went to speak with the child's parents about this incident. Altering such behavior, however, demands a major cultural change!

"The authorities do far too little about the criminality against Jews. One New Year's Eve, hooligans shouted in front of my house, 'Jews Jews' and started to destroy my gate. I called the police, who arrived an hour and a half later.

"The Board of the Rabbinate decided that I need to have an alarm system at home which is connected directly to the police station. Initially I thought this was nonsense. But the system was put in nevertheless. I am not afraid, but it surprised me that I felt more secure with the alarm. This feeling in itself frightened me. I don't go to bed anymore without putting the alarm on.

"A major problem for the Jewish community is that the Dutch media is also anti-Israeli. They use expressions which are a new type of anti-Semitism. I try to correct that as much as possible.

"I remember a big photograph in the local newspaper *Amersfoortse Courant* of an Israeli tank. The article said that it had run over and killed a Palestinian. Next to it was a small news item about how during that same week in another country, 200 executions had taken place.

"I asked the editors: 'Why do you devote a quarter of a page to a dead Palestinian and only a small article to 200 dead people elsewhere?' They replied: 'We don't have a journalist in that country.' Just to clarify, I believe that one Palestinian killed is one too many. Afterwards, however, it turned out that he had not been killed, nor had the tank run him over."

The Netherlands Should Apologize
to the Jewish Community

D R. ELS BORST-EILERS was minister of public health, well-being, and
sport from 1994 to 2002 and also deputy prime minister for the last
four years. She says about her background: "I was eight years old when the
Germans invaded our country in 1940 and thirteen when they were ejected.
At that age you are already aware of many things. I have always lived in
Amsterdam. During the war, we inhabited the Rivieren neighborhood
where many Jews lived at the time. Our downstairs neighbors were Jews,
and there were also Jews a few houses from us. We saw how they were
rounded up and taken away. That made a strong impression on me."

*"If I had been prime minister, I would have offered apologies to the Dutch
Jewish community without hesitation. This would refer both to our government's
attitude during the Second World War and to the very late postwar discovery
that the restitution process had been poorly conceived."*

Borst says: "We now know that the persecution of the Dutch Jews hardly
bothered Queen Wilhelmina in her London exile. She spoke all the time
about the heroes of the resistance and thought that the entire Netherlands
was resisting. The Queen spoke in a manner of 'all of you who fight so
courageously,' which was far from the truth.

"The weak Dutch government in exile in London should not have left everything to the Queen. Prime Minister Pieter Gerbrandy should have addressed the population on the radio to the effect that 'we expect you to protect your fellow Jewish citizens from deportation. Try to take them into your homes, help them to flee, do whatever you can. You must do something for our fellow citizens.'

"My feeling is that if all Catholics or Reformed Christians had been deported to Germany, the Dutch government in London would have instructed the population in the occupied Netherlands to help them. The government's attitude testified that its members, like many others, saw the Jewish Dutchmen as a special group who were not 'real Dutchmen.'

"Before the war, many Dutchmen thought the 140,000 Jews among them were a group that should be watched. They might be a threat—for instance, they might get the good jobs, or aspire to dominance in the financial world. These people were parroting each other with no knowledge of the facts.

"This lack of interest in the fate of the Jews was a consequence of pre-war anti-Semitism in the Netherlands. It also existed in my nice family. I had a fully Jewish uncle who had married my aunt. At the beginning of the war, he divorced his wife in order to save her from danger. He thereby endangered himself as he was then no longer in a mixed marriage. He was hidden all throughout the war and fortunately enough survived. Our entire family was happy about this.

"Yet before the war, for instance at family gatherings for a birthday, it was quite common to hear comments such as 'a typical Jewish trick' or 'the Jews take good care of themselves.' That was when someone had done something smart with money. I noticed this already as a small child.

"None of us would have wanted to do any evil to a Jew. Yet there was a feeling of 'they have done very well financially' despite the fact that there were many very poor Jews in Amsterdam."

Borst sees parallels between the war years, her time in the government, and current Dutch politics. She was a minister at the time of the mass murder in the Bosnian town of Srebrenica and also when the results of the subsequent inquiry by the Dutch Institute for War Documentation (NIOD) were published in 2002. The NIOD claimed in its report that when the Dutch government decided to recall the Dutch United Nations soldiers from Srebrenica, it did not know of the dangers to the Bosnian citizens. Borst remarks: "The NIOD embellished what had happened."

After Minister Jan Pronk of the Labor Party said the government had actually known what was happening in Srebrenica and about the dangers to the citizens there, Borst confirmed that this was true.

As far as the present is concerned, Borst says: "There are many nice, peaceful Muslims, but the Netherlands is far too tolerant regarding the statements of the radical wing of Islam. This also concerns Moroccan youngsters who make anti-Semitic remarks or commit anti-Semitic acts. They were not born as Jew-haters, but they live in a culture where this is tolerated or even encouraged."

She concludes: "There is much cover-up in the Netherlands in the name of a multicultural society. Ayaan Hirsi Ali made this very clear many times. She was very right about this."

Identifying with Israel Makes Me Jewish

LEON DE WINTER was born in 1954. He is one of the Netherlands' best-known writers. For several years he was associated with the Hudson Institute think tank. In 2006, he was awarded the Buber-Rosenzweig Medal in Germany for his battle against anti-Semitic and racist attitudes in society.

"The Netherlands is to a certain extent a decadent country, in particular if one observes Dutch society. In the 1960s, a process started in which all forms of deviant behavior that one could imagine were openly tolerated. Normative behavior—civil decency—has been lost."

De Winter remarks: "I am a Dutchman and I very much like the Netherlands, its craziness, its contradictions, and the schizophrenia. On the one hand, it has a strong Calvinist slant in combination with an almost anarchistic tolerance. Dutch Society continuously seeks equilibrium and has many faces, which makes it very interesting.

"Identifying with Israel makes me Jewish. I am not religious, but I clearly show where my sympathies lie in the Palestinian-Israeli conflict. I think that many people take that as a sign of my Jewishness."

De Winter claims that he doesn't care about "extreme reactions" to what he says. "When I have participated in a debate about Israel on TV, I do not want to know about the emails the station receives in response. I know that there are many negative remarks about me on Moroccan, Muslim, and neo-Nazi websites, but I'm not going to search for them.

"I also do not frequent places where a confrontation could take place. On the trains, I am sometimes cursed at by Moroccan youngsters who want to provoke a Dutch passenger if they see that he or she doesn't like their noise-making, for instance."

About Israel, De Winter says: "A number of Dutchmen who are part of the political establishment express sentiments which they call anti-Zionist, while at the same time they will claim, 'But I am not an anti-Semite.' Whoever is obsessed with the fate of the Palestinians, which is relatively light compared to that of many others, also suffers from an excessive interest in Jews. For anti-Semites, 'Zionism' becomes a cover to express themselves negatively about Jews.

"It is intriguing how these problems have become an obsession for some people. The non-Jewish Dutchman can choose to focus on many different sufferings in the world. It could very well be that people know that this particular conflict will always draw attention.

"In the Netherlands there is a small anti-Israeli Jewish organization called Another Jewish Voice. They continuously claim: 'We Jews have lived through the Shoah and have an obligation to exhibit the highest morals.' They present the Shoah as an educational institute for Jews to teach Jewish morals. In other words, the Nazis held courses in the concentration camps in order to imbue Jews with humanity. These are Jews who pervert the memory of the Shoah. It is a noisy group which attracts much media attention because its conveys a message which many non-Jews like to hear.

"The Dutch newspapers put Israel on the front page all the time—as if what happens there is the most important thing in the world. The mass murders in Darfur and Congo with their huge death counts in recent years are apparently irrelevant because the newspapers write very little about them.

"The radio and TV have created intense images. One sees in the Netherlands an enormous change in the depiction of Israel in the past twenty-five years. The media has been influenced by news sent back home by Dutch correspondents in the Middle East and the filtered information. It is also related to changes in democratic attitudes and the immigration of North African and Turkish Muslims to the Netherlands and Europe.

"The classic hard-core anti-Semitism among North Africans in the Netherlands is very worrying. It is related to the identification of Moroccan youngsters with Palestinians and with viewpoints that are part of traditional Islam. Yet in the Dutch community, there also remain stereotypes about Jews."

De Winter concludes: "What is happening in the Netherlands and Europe is a prelude of terrible things to come. The great story of the love Jews have for Europe has come to an end. In this sense, the Nazis have been successful. The presence of Jews in Europe will end.

"Instead of restless, difficult, creative, funny, and smart Jews, Europe has imported Muslims who are generally poorly educated and frequently frustrated, aggressive, and destructive. I have written about these issues for years already. But people only start to understand it a little bit when something dramatic happens such as the murder of the Dutch media maker Theo van Gogh or the suicide attacks in London."

Distorted Dutch Views of the Jews

ELMA DRAYER worked at the Dutch daily *Trouw* from 2001 until 2010. She started as an editor and thereafter became a columnist. Now she is a freelance journalist.

"September 11, 2001, was a turning point in the Netherlands. In the following weeks, there was unrest in Amsterdam West where many Muslims live. Around that time I was writing an article about a small synagogue in that part of town. A few weeks later, Moroccan youngsters threw stones at Jews who came out of the synagogue. I called the police to check what was happening. The police spokesman said: 'I would prefer if you don't give too much attention to this. These people are already in an unfavorable position.' He wasn't speaking about the Jews at whom the stones were thrown, but about the Muslims who threw the stones. Perpetrators thus became victims and victims became perpetrators."

Drayer says that this anecdote must be seen in a larger context. "In recent years, one hears public statements which were deemed socially unacceptable in the Netherlands after the Second World War. After the war, however, anti-Semitism was heavily suppressed. Now people speak about the Jews in an increasingly condescending way. This is also related to the changed position of Israel. One cannot separate the anti-Israel mood from anti-Semitism.

"To this has to be added that many people do not take Muslims seriously but view them with pity. This is a new form of the ancient paternalism. Yet if one states that this construct plays a major role in judgment about Israel, one receives reactions like: 'You are never allowed to say something about Israel because then you are immediately termed an anti-Semite.'

"In a column about the conference of Holocaust deniers in Tehran in 2006, I wrote: 'Maybe I missed it, but I haven't seen any angry Jews shouting in our streets marching toward the Iranian Embassy. I didn't hear them chant: "All Muslims are liars." Nowhere have I seen an effigy of Ahmadinejad in flames. Yet, this conference was an incredible provocation. On the other hand, the Muslim world requires far less provocation in order to explode. One only has to remember the reactions to the Muhammed cartoons.'

"In 2007, a report from the Center for Information and Documentation on Israel (CIDI) was published. It gave a nuanced view of anti-Semitic incidents in the Netherlands which had increased in 2006 by 64 percent. The three main national 'quality' papers, of which my own is one, didn't publish this information. I wrote a column about that. One of my colleagues was very angry that I had written that the report hadn't been mentioned in our paper. He said that CIDI was a Jewish lobbying organization—which I had explicitly mentioned—and that the data weren't so bad. This kind of totally unfounded statement would never have been made about any other monitor of racism. As soon as it concerns Jews, the report is suddenly 'subjective and unreliable.' After such a trying day, I had to seek support from one of the few journalists at the paper who shared my views. Sometimes I felt very lonely working there.

"When the tree which Anne Frank saw from her hiding place almost collapsed in 2007—in 2010 it actually fell over—a national debate took place. I wrote that we in the Netherlands grant honor to dead Jews. We, however, don't want much contact with living Jews, especially those in Israel.

"What I write about Israel is apparently not considered a normal opinion. People often say: 'Mrs. Drayer, you must be Jewish.' They think that only Jews can voice positions like I do. I would consider it an honor to be Jewish, but I'm not. I just express my points of view. I have even heard colleagues say that Jewish journalists should not write about non-Western immigrants because they are prejudiced. I consider that statement very anti-Semitic. On the other hand, I receive many positive reactions from readers, which offers a welcome balance.

"I've read the Hamas Charter which promotes the murder of all Jews. Yet people do not care to find out what is written in it. One of the oft-heard comparisons in the Netherlands is that of Jews and Muslims. A false impression is given that Muslims are similarly the victims of the Dutch people as the Jews once were. It is expressed as: 'Islamophobia is the new anti-Semitism.'

"For many years now, I have lived near a synagogue in Amsterdam. When there are services on Saturdays, police are on guard. This doesn't shock anyone in the neighborhood. Yet it is a scandal that this is necessary."

Short Stories about
Amsterdam Anti-Semitism

CHARLES DAHAN, an Amsterdam wine trader, was born in Marrakesh in Morocco. His mother tongue is Arabic. In 1956, he immigrated to France at the age of twenty. Later on, he married a Dutch-Jewish woman and moved to Amsterdam.

"One Yom Kippur, I walked out of the beautiful Amsterdam Portuguese synagogue together with a law professor. In front of the nearby Jewish Historical Museum, some Moroccan boys were singing in Arabic with a nice melody. The professor said, 'Look at those kids.' He remarked on how pleasant their singing was.

"I said, 'You don't know what they're singing! The words are 'Here come the Jews, Death to the Jews! We will get them.' He remarked, 'That's impossible. Look how nice they are!' I got very angry, but Dutchmen are naïve and don't want to believe what happens right in front of their eyes."

Dahan observes: "My experiences are like short stories, nothing special, but often based on the fact that I understand Arabic. A few years ago, the sewer in front of our house broke down. The municipality sent workers to repair it. One of them was an Arab. When I passed, I spoke to him in Arabic. I asked him whether he wanted a cup of coffee. I brought it to him. He said: 'In Amsterdam, the Jews are the boss and we even have a Jewish mayor.' I replied: 'Well, I have to leave for work now.' I took the empty cup and closed the door."

Dahan continues: "If there are anti-Semites in Amsterdam among Muslim immigrants and if they make anti-Semitic remarks in school, that is not of their own initiative. They have never seen Jews before. It doesn't matter whether they were born here or in the Rif Mountains in Morocco where there are hardly any Jews left. They learned anti-Semitism from their parents at home, or from watching satellite TV.

"The problem of anti-Semitism in the Netherlands does not only involve Muslims. A Dutch medical doctor who lives on my street visited me often because he liked to drink wine. When his daughter married an Iraqi Arab, he told me: 'My daughter brought a Jew home.' I said: 'What do you mean a Jew? He's an Iraqi Muslim and Arab—why do you call him a Jew?' He said: 'It's all the same—to me he's a Jew.' He knew that I am Jewish, but he drank a bit too much."

Dahan continued: "I once had a textile wholesaler as a client. He always bought wine wholesale. Whenever a client came to him, he opened a bottle before they spoke business. The client drinks a bit, buys a bit, it's a very good way of marketing the wine—the better for him, the better for me.

"One day he came along with three or four friends. I let them taste some wines. He said: 'I brought you some new clients—friends from my youth. They love wine as much as I do. Show us something.' They wanted to sing something and I said: 'Please, go ahead.'

"They started to sing Nazi songs. I said: 'What are you singing? Are you crazy?' They said: 'We all belong to the same club.' It turned out that they had all been Nazi collaborators. I said: 'Stop singing! You know that I am Jewish! And if you want to order something, send me the order by fax or phone. Goodbye.'

"This textile wholesaler was very polite. I have a *mezuzah* on my door. The first time he visited me he said when he saw it: 'Did you buy this apartment from a Jew?' I answered: 'I don't know who the previous owner was nor whether he was Jewish.' He pointed to the *mezuzah* and said: 'Only Jews have that on their door.' Then I told him: 'I'm Jewish and I put it there.'

"It didn't bother him. He found my prices and the wines attractive. When he came here, he drank as much as he wanted. But when he got drunk that time, it was very clear what he was thinking. I never did business with him again.

"Fifteen years ago, I had a bonded warehouse for wine in the Amsterdam harbor. A Dutchman also had a warehouse next to mine. Every morning he said to me: 'Have you decided to leave for Israel yet?' I asked him: 'Why are you asking me that?' He said: 'Because I need your warehouse.' I ignored him, but then one day he said to me: 'The Jews have no business being in Israel, it belongs to the Arabs.'"

Dahan concludes: "These are all little Amsterdam stories."

Jews and Anti-Semitism in Switzerland

S IMON ERLANGER is a journalist and historian. He was born in Switzerland in 1965 and educated in Basel and Jerusalem. He teaches Jewish history at the University of Lucerne and also works as an editor for a television station in northwestern Switzerland.

"There are about eighteen thousand Jews in Switzerland. This is about the same number as in 1900. The general population, however, has more than doubled since then to over 7.8 million. The number of Swiss Jews and their descendants living in Israel is fourteen thousand. Since it was usually the young and active who left for Israel, the Swiss Jewish community today tends to be older with many members on the periphery of the communities.

"Demographically, Jewish life is centered today in Zurich and to lesser extent in Geneva and Basel. Only in Zurich the number of Jews remains constant at about six thousand. The Basel Jewish community, for instance, has diminished by about a third in the past thirty years and now numbers around 1,100. Many small communities had already vanished by the 1990s and others are likely to disappear within a generation."

Erlanger says: "Following the Six-Day War, the anti-Zionism of the New Left became a political factor in Switzerland overriding the traditional pro-Israel stance of the social-democratic left. Anti-Semitic incidents were rare during the 1970s but began to multiply after the Lebanon War of 1982. By then, for example, cemeteries were desecrated almost on a regular basis. During the 1980s and 1990s a militant extreme Right also emerged. Due to the country's liberal laws, Holocaust deniers and revisionists used Switzerland as a base. This changed for the better by 1994 with the introduction of an 'anti-racism law.'

"By 1987 when the First Intifada broke out, most of the Swiss mainstream media had become hostile toward Israel, and the general atmosphere for Jews had deteriorated. Since then, Switzerland has seen an unprecedented upsurge of both traditional anti-Semitism and its newer disguise 'anti-Israelism.'

"A 2007 poll found that over 86 percent of Swiss Jews deplore media bias and distortions. They consider that this has contributed to a major decrease in personal and communal security. There are many verbal and sometimes physical attacks. They are rarely recorded. In 2007, the SIG, the Swiss Federation of Jewish Communities, set up an institution to collect data and provide statistics. Another organization, CICAD, reports on anti-Semitic incidents in the western, French-speaking part of Switzerland. Most Swiss Jewish communities employ important security measures.

"A specific Swiss element in the rise in anti-Semitism was the affair of the dormant Jewish bank accounts during 1992–1998. For many years, descendants of Holocaust victims had claimed accounts that their murdered relatives had held in Swiss banks. This issue was raised immediately after the war and then again in the 1950s. After payment of small sums by the banks to Jewish organizations and the Swiss Federation of Jewish Communities, the matter had been considered settled.

"Restitution issues were reopened in Europe in the 1990s. Concerning Switzerland, this developed into a controversy about the country's record during the Second World War. This included economic collaboration with the Nazis, laundering of stolen gold, and the anti-Jewish refugee policy. The government initially refused to cooperate with Jewish claimants as did the banks. Later on, major Jewish organizations and the US government became involved. This led to the worst Swiss foreign policy crisis in decades. Ultimately, a financial settlement was reached between Swiss banks and Jewish organizations.

"The Swiss then had to face a past that did not correspond to the heroic self-image they had cherished. The myth of neutrality while at the same time resisting Nazi Germany was largely discarded. Many Swiss felt coerced by a hostile outside world—mainly Jews and Americans—seeking to damage Switzerland's self-image for political and financial purposes. Thereupon a sizable rise occurred in anti-Semitism and anti-Americanism.

"In 1996, then-Swiss President Pascal Delamuraz referred to the restitution debate as blackmail and asked whether Auschwitz was located in Switzerland. This gave anti-Semitism a new respectability. The debate on the Swiss wartime record relegitimized anti-Semitism in many parts of society and unleashed an anti-Semitic wave.

"There was another anti-Semitic wave in 2001. Then-Economics Minister, Federal Counselor Pascale Couchepin suggested, along with the Swiss Federation of Jewish Communities, to abolish the prohibition of *shechita* (ritual slaughter). Not only militant animal rights groups, but much of the public was outraged by this proposal. Articles and letters to the editor openly used traditional anti-Semitic language that would have been unacceptable earlier. The government dropped the proposal to keep internal peace."

Concerning the future, Erlanger concludes: "Many young Swiss Jews have emigrated over the decades, while many others have opted out of the organized Jewish community and often out of any form of Jewish life. The future of the community—however well established and affluent—is cause for concern."

Belgian Anti-Semitism and Anti-Zionism

A NDRE GANTMAN is a Jewish jurist. He is a former alderman in Antwerp on behalf of the Liberal Party (VLD). In 2011 he wrote a book about anti-Semitism called *The Split Conscience*.

"For many years, images from Auschwitz had constrained public expression of anti-Semitism. However, anti-Semitic thoughts have remained in the minds of many. As is often the case elsewhere, anti-Semitism and anti-Zionism in Belgium are practiced by many. It is found among politicians, media, trade unions, academics, NGOs, and so on. This is true for both French-speaking Wallonia and Dutch-speaking Flanders."

Gantman says: "Belgian authorities subsidize several organizations which promote an economic and academic boycott of Israel. These include international bodies such as the Catholic Pax Christi and the development aid organization Oxfam. The extreme anti-Israel author Luc Catherine—author of the book *The Israel Lobby*—claims that there is no pro-Palestinian lobby in Flanders. He is right, because there is mainly an anti-Israel lobby which demonizes Israel.

"The Socialist Trade Union (ABVV) is a major initiator of anti-Israelism. The ABVV wants to exclude the Israeli Histadrut from the international trade union organization. Bias is easy to see. Belgian Socialist Prime Minister Elio Di Rupo is vice chairman of the Socialist International. The parties of the deposed Tunisian and Egyptian dictators were members there until the so-called Arab Spring.

"One finds radical anti-Israelis among politicians from many parties. An extreme one is Eva Brems, a federal parliamentarian from the Flemish Green Party. She is a former chair of Amnesty International in Flanders. Rarely a week passes by without her posing provocative questions with an anti-Israel slant to ministers.

"The French-speaking Free University of Brussels is yet another major center of anti-Semitism. Jacques Brotchi, a Jewish professor of medicine and senator of the Wallonian Liberal Party (MR) resigned from the board of this university last year because of the escalating anti-Semitism there.

"At the Flemish-speaking Free University of Brussels, the annual Boycott Israel Week took place. The European Union of Arab Students was one of the organizers of a lecture by Azzan Tamimi, a supporter of the Muslim Brotherhood. The university administration requested that a pro-Israeli speaker also be invited to speak after Tamimi. Tamimi, who publicly supports terrorism and suicide bombings against Israel, left after his own speech. A few days later, he spoke on Al Jazeera against freedom and democracy.

"From time to time, Muslim anti-Semitism reaches extreme proportions. In 2009, I spoke at the University of Antwerp. A young Muslim dressed up in white asked me: 'Does human blood flow through your veins?' His attempts to dehumanize me reminded me of Nazi ideology.

"Anti-Semitism has also spread among the younger generation of Muslims. A study published in 2011 by Professor Marc Elchardus of The Flemish Free University of Brussels shows that Muslim anti-Semitism at Brussels Dutch-speaking schools by far exceeds that of other students.

About 50 percent of Muslim students harbor anti-Semitic sentiments. For other students it is 10 percent. The study also shows that there is far more anti-Semitism than anti-Muslim feelings.

"Generally speaking, Belgian authorities underestimate the negative attitude of Muslims toward Jews. In the past, they were obsessed by the idea that criticizing this kind of anti-Semitism, as well as pinpointing Islam extremism, would encourage racism against Muslims. Consequently, the so-called 'multicultural society' would be severely battered. In 2010, the Belgian federal government organized a round table discussion on multiculturalism. From the report on the discussions, it became clear that those present were willing to partially abandon the basic values which democratic societies have acquired through great sacrifice over the centuries.

"Participants indicated that equality for citizens, the battle against racism and xenophobia, and the equality of men and women are not absolute values. They seem to think that a compromise which includes other values has to be found. This is derived from the incorrect idea that the fundamentals of a democratic society should be adapted to the values held by newcomers, i.e. the Muslims. Not surprisingly, there was also a recommendation made to cancel the law which makes Holocaust denial punishable."

Gantman also focuses on mainstream political correctness: "Many anti-Israelis apply double standards. This became most clear from their responses when the Goldstone Report was published. Israel-haters usually turn their heads away when extreme war crimes and crimes against humanity are committed in many other countries. Of course when Goldstone changed his opinion in 2011 in favor of Israel, he was accused of being a Zionist.

"By and large it can also be stated that the media tend to bash Israel. For instance, very often when the Israel Air Force launches a defensive action against armed groups in Gaza, it is hardly mentioned that Israeli cities were previously under attack by rockets fired from there."

Gantman concludes: "There is a glimmer of hope though. Minister of Justice Annemie Turtelboom appointed a special prosecutor to coordinate police actions to fight anti-Semitism."

Anti-Semitism and Anti-Israelism
in the Czech Republic

I vo Cerman is an assistant professor of history at the University of South Bohemia in Budweis. He focuses on the history of the Enlightenment and human rights. He has also published studies on early modern anti-Semitism.

"The most dangerous expressions of classic anti-Semitism in the Czech Republic are found on the Internet—on neo-Nazi websites such as Národní vzdělávací institut (National Institute of Education). Extreme leftist websites which attack Israel base their arguments on the defense of human rights. There are no anti-Jewish riots or similar grave incidents in the country. Some incidents such as insulting Jews, or graffiti on Jewish property have been recorded by the police and by the Security Center of the Jewish Community. Hate graffiti on synagogues or Jewish homes is usually removed quickly.

"Vandalism in Jewish cemeteries—such as the much-publicized case in Puklice in 2012—is rarely connected with anti-Semitism. In 2008, bronze plaques from tombstones in the former concentration camp Theresienstadt were stolen. The thieves wanted to sell the bronze and did not act out of anti-Semitic motives. These plaques have since then been replaced with plastic imitations."

Cerman remarks: "News coverage on Israel in the mainstream Czech media is very biased. This developed mainly after the Second Lebanon War in 2006. It further increased after the Cast Lead Campaign against Hamas in 2008 and 2009. The Gaza flotilla incident in May 2010 became another turning point. Czech National TV sent journalist Petr Zavadil as an official participant in the flotilla. He was accompanied by cameraman Jan Línek and the independents Zdeněk Lokaj, a jourmalist, and Alexandr Vojta, a movie maker. All four were subsequently arrested and deported by the IDF.

"They published their experiences posing as 'heroes of the struggle for human rights.' Línek initially claimed falsely that Israeli soldiers were firing at them with live ammunition. He and the others were however not on the *Mavi Marmara*, the only ship where fighting took place. The representatives of the Czech National TV issued public statements in which they accused the IDF of torture and inhumane treatment. Zavadil had also misinformed the public during Operation Cast Lead, when he aired a series of reports in which he announced the most hideous crimes as 'true facts' committed by Israeli soldiers.

"Czech National TV covered the flotilla with a very anti-Israeli slant. Many official Israeli rebuttals were disregarded outright, while Turkish and Hamas opinions were presented as facts. The public was incited to hatred with the airing of coffins of dead Turkish activists and emotional reports about the suffering of their relatives on TV. The suffering of Israelis in Sderot had been mentioned only in two reports by Jakub Szántó in December 2008.

"Some representatives of the older generation of Communist propaganda journalism returned onto the scene. One was the former TV reporter and Communist diplomat Ivan Brož, who passed away in 2012. He published a book on Israel's wars, in which he brands Jewish settlers of the 1930s and 1940s as 'terrorists.'

"Extreme leftist movements easily infiltrate academia and political parties. Political scientist Marek Čejka, from Brno University, wrote several biased books on Israeli history. Political scientist Pavel Barša, from Charles University in Prague, organized a lecture by Holocaust distorter Norman Finkelstein.

"Several anti-Israel rallies and campaigns have been organized by the Czech section of the International Solidarity Movement (ISM), which probably consists of one person. Yet the ISM has a circle of collaborators who, along with significant leftist politicians, joined these rallies and signed petitions against Israel.

"In the past, the major Czech parties either supported Israel or avoided the topic. More recently, however, some representatives of the Czech Social Democrat Party have publicly supported the Palestinians and attacked Israel.

"The significance of Arab diplomacy should not be understated. Palestinian Ambassador Mohamed Salaymeh participated in anti-Israel rallies and gave lectures at universities. Saudi Arabia has great influence on the Czech Muslim community due to its financial power. One organization it sponsors is The Islamic Foundation in Brno, which promotes radical Islam.

"Lukáš Větrovec is a young Czech convert to Islam and preacher in Brno. In December 2011, a recording of his sermon was leaked to the media. He accused Israel of genocide against the Palestinian people, compared the Gaza Strip to 'one huge concentration camp,' and incited hatred against Jews. His sermon received sharp criticism from the Federation of Jewish Communities, which represents the three thousand organized Jews in the Czech Republic.

"There are about 11,000 Muslims in the country, a recent phenomenon. In the population census only 3,600 declared themselves as such. A significant number of Czech converts to Islam actively spread radical Islamism. The Islamic Foundation and their collaborating organizations promote anti-Jewish hatred at schools, public rallies, on the Internet, and in their publications.

"There are about three thousand to five thousand supporters of neo-Nazi movements. They organized two big anti-Israel campaigns and are active on the Internet. They hope that anti-Roma feelings will help them win popular support. Neo-Nazi's are not yet a major threat, as they are not backed by any significant political party."

Argentina, Jews, and Israel

D**R. G**USTAVO **P**EREDNIK **is the author of fifteen books on Jews and modernity. He has lectured in fifty countries on Jews, Jewish civilization, and Israel. He was in charge of the four-year program for foreign students at the Hebrew University Rothberg School and was head of the Jerusalem Institute for Youth Leaders.**

"The Jewish community in Argentina numbers an estimated 150,000. It has declined from double that figure half a century ago, due to emigration and assimilation. Over 80 percent of the country's Jews live in Buenos Aires.

"In my opinion, current Judeophobia—a term which I prefer over the misleading 'anti-Semitism'—expresses itself mainly in three ways. The first is the delegitimization of Israel in publications, public statements, and demonstrations. The second is through Judeophobic individuals and organizations which are close to the country's centers of power. In Argentina, one example of this is trade union militant Luis D'Elía, an Iran apologist who in 2012 publicly blamed the Mossad for a huge case of corruption in Argentina. The third way is the recurrence of classic Judeophobic myths in mainstream discourse, among them that Jews have 'excessive power' and trivializing the Shoah."

Dr. Perednik observes: "We find persistent hatred of Israel in the left-wing media, such as the daily *Página/12*. The same goes for part of academia. Some well-known professors are rabidly anti-Zionist. So are large segments of the very often leftist student organizations. Many of their leaders are Jews.

"The Jewish community umbrella organization DAIA annually publishes a compendium of anti-Jewish aggression. It mentions regular verbal attacks in neo-Nazi style radio programs such as *Alerta Nacional* and *Juventud Despierta*, as well as in magazines such as the Catholic right wing *Cabildo*—which is nostalgic for the dictatorship of the generals—and *Patria Argentina*. In recent years, Judeophobic expressions have been decreasing, however. Judeophobic graffiti also declined by one third in 2011 compared to 2010.

"On the radical Left there is the Quebracho group, which frequently calls Israel a 'Nazi-state.' It often disrupts solidarity meetings with Israel. Several of its members have been jailed for beating demonstrators. Quebracho can be considered an Iranian voice in Argentina.

"In 2012, a book titled *The Rabbis of Malvinas* was published. It revealed virulent cases of Judeophobia by army officers during Argentina's 1982 war against the United Kingdom. Jewish soldiers who suffered insults, humiliations, and beatings were only honored by Jewish organizations thirty years later.

"Argentinian politicians are careful not to use bigoted language against Jews or others. Foreign Minister Hector Timerman is Jewish and has close family in Israel. Several important supporters of the government publicly identify as Jews.

"The government's actions show a clear intention to denounce Judeophobia. A much publicized act was the expulsion of Holocaust denier and dissident Catholic Bishop Williamson in 2009. Yet because of Argentina's close ties with Venezuelan President Hugo Chavez, the government does not oppose the delegitimization of Israel. In general, the Argentine government is very tough on nationalistic Judeophobia from the extreme Right and oblivious to anti-Zionistic Judeophobia from the extreme Left.

"At the beginning of December 2012, Ecuador's President Rafael Correa—a Chavez ally—visited Argentina. Besides defending the Iranian government, he disparaged the largest terrorist attack ever in Argentina's history. In 1994, Iran-sponsored terrorists bombed the building which housed the Jewish AMIA organization in Buenos Aires, killing 85 and wounding hundreds.

"Correa declared at a press conference during his visit that 'the AMIA case was very painful for Argentine history. But only God knows how many civilians died in the NATO bombings in Libya. Therefore, we should compare and let's see where the real dangers are.' He also said later that there was nothing he should apologize for.

"This statement went unchallenged by the Argentine government. It is evidently seeking to get closer to Iran. Its motives are economic as well as staying in line with Chavez's views. My book *To Kill Without a Trace* (2009) which deals with Iranian terrorist acts in Argentina, foresaw that the government would zigzag toward Iran. The judicial investigations have shown convincingly that Iran was behind the AMIA attack and the 1992 car bombing of the Israeli Embassy in which more than 20 people were killed and close to 250 wounded. Yet Argentina never severed diplomatic relations with Iran.

"The Iranian government has thus succeeded in transforming a legal case into a political negotiation. Argentina, probably inspired by Chavez, is currently negotiating with the perpetrators about how to 'solve' the most deadly terror attacks 'issue' ever committed in Argentina.

"Jewish community representatives are in regular contact with the government. Their agenda, however, is not always clear. Many pressing issues of Judeophobia in Argentina remain unaddressed. For example, Jewish leaders did not complain to the government about its condoning of Correa's comments, nor about its open friendship with the Judeophobe Chavez."

The Uncertain Future
of Turkey's Jewish Community

R IFAT N. BALI is an independent scholar. He is a research fellow of the Alberto Benveniste Center for Sephardic Studies and Culture in Paris. Bali is the author of numerous books and articles on the history of Turkish Jewry.

"The Jewish community in Turkey is one of the few surviving ones in a Muslim country. Its numbers have, however, dwindled greatly. In 1927, the Turkish Republic conducted its first general census which found that there were 81,872 Jews. After Israel's independence in 1948, about half of Turkey's Jews left for Israel. In following years, emigration continued parallel to political and economic turbulences. The present number of Jews is somewhere between sixteen thousand and twenty thousand."

Bali says: "In recent years, the Jewish community has become the target of much hostility and verbal abuse by the country's Islamic and ultra-nationalist sectors. Zionism and Israel are publicly demonized and this sentiment often crosses the line into anti-Semitism. It is unthinkable that any Turkish Jew would make pro-Israel statements openly to correct all the misinformation and disinformation concerning Israel and Zionism."

"On May 31, 2010, the Israeli Defense Forces stopped the Turkish *Mavi Marmara* ship of the flotilla of the Free Gaza Movement and the Turkish Foundation for Human Rights and Freedom and Humanitarian Relief (IHH). In the ensuing fight, eight Turkish nationals and one Turkish American were killed.

"This became a critical moment for the Jewish community. The Turkish public perceived the incident as the murder of Muslim Turks by the Jewish army. A new wave of anti-Semitism and conspiracy theories appeared in the Turkish media and were supported by public figures. One conspiracy theory was that Israel was behind the separatist Kurdistan Workers Party's (PKK) attack on a Turkish military base which occurred a few hours after the IDF intervention on the *Mavi Marmara*.

"It came as no surprise that the Turkish media would ask Jewish leaders to declare which side they were on. The chief rabbinate responded a few hours after the incident saying: 'We are distressed to learn of the military intervention carried out against the ship *Mavi Marmara* which was heading toward Gaza. The fact that, according to the first reports we have received, there have been dead and wounded in the intervention, has increased our sorrow all the more. We fully share our country's reaction generated by the stopping of the aforementioned [relief] effort in this manner, and our sorrow is the same as that of the general public.'

"Besides this declaration, the Jewish community tried to keep as low a profile as possible. This void was filled by two Turkish Jewish public figures. Mario Levi is a well-known novelist. He told the Italian daily *La Repubblica* that 'As Jews in Istanbul, we are in solidarity with the people in Gaza.' He added that he did not think there was anti-Semitism in Turkey.

"Roni Margulies is a Jewish Trotskyite poet and a columnist at the liberal-leftist daily *Taraf*. He stated that he approved of the Gaza flotilla, disapproved of Israel's raid, and wished he could have been there. He remarked that 'For a Jew, Israel is the most dangerous place to live in the world and Israel is a danger to world Jewry.' Both Levi and Margulies' statements were well received by the Turkish media. The *Mavi Marmara* incident has thus shown again that the Turkish public and media see an anti-Zionist as a good Jew and a pro-Zionist as a bad Jew.

"In such an environment, the leadership of the Turkish Jewish community cannot reach out to Turkish society. In order to preserve the identity of the Turkish Jewish youth, Zionism and an attachment to Israel are two main themes taught to them. Jewish parents, however, counsel their children not to display Star of David necklaces in public and to ignore as much as possible the hateful criticism of Israel in the Turkish public sphere.

"The Turkish Jewish community has one element of added value for the government. It is expected to help convince American Jewish organizations to use their influence to block the official recognition as genocide by the US Congress of the 1915 murderous deportation by the Ottoman Turks of the Armenians.

"In the past decades, there has been increased violence toward the Jewish community. There was an assassination attempt against Jak V. Kamhi in 1993, the president of the Quincentennial Foundation and a prominent businessman. The Foundation was established in 1989 to celebrate the quincentennial anniversary of the arrival of Sephardi Jews to Ottoman lands. In 1995, there was an attempt against the president of Ankara's small Jewish community, Professor Yuda Yürüm. Yasef Yahya, an Istanbul dentist, was murdered in 2003. Later that year, there were two suicide bomb attacks by radical Islamists against two Istanbul synagogues, Neve Shalom and Beth Israel."

Bali concludes: "The long-term viability of the Turkish Jewish community is doubtful. Its influence in society is negligible. It plays no role in the country's cultural, political, or intellectual life. There is no one in Turkish civil society to respond to the widespread, hostile rhetoric. The Jewish community is therefore totally dependent on the government to protect its members."

Libyan Jews Watching Post-Qaddafi Libya

P ROFESSOR MAURICE ROUMANI, a world expert on Libyan Jewry, taught politics and the Middle East at Ben-Gurion University in Beer Sheva and is the founding director of the J.R. Elyachar Center for Sephardi Studies there. The latest of his many books is *The Jews of Libya: Coexistence, Persecution, Resettlement* (2008).

"Libyan Jews almost unanimously greeted the fall of Muammar Qaddafi believing that he deserved his fate. Qaddafi was notorious for being anti-Israeli. With regard to Libyan Jews in Italy, he played games of being close at times, while distant on other occasions. On his last visit to Rome in 2010, Qaddafi was only willing to meet the Jews during the Sabbath. He was well aware that such a meeting would be humiliating, as the Jews would have to desecrate their holy day. Only a few women met with him. They were later condemned by most of the community.

"Qaddafi had promised compensation for the huge collective and private property which the Jews left behind when forced to flee Libya. He never delivered, however. Qaddafi also invited Jews to return to Libya, which they regarded as a ploy. All they wanted was to recover their possessions or to renew business ties with Libya."

Roumani observes: "The great majority of Libyan Jews now lives in Israel. They regarded Qaddafi's fall as an even more positive event than Libyan Jews elsewhere—mainly in Italy, the United States, and the United Kingdom. Qaddafi had repeatedly invited his former countrymen in Israel to come back to Libya thus allowing the Palestinians to regain Palestine. Qaddafi was also a terrorism supporter.

"The general consensus among Libyan Jews toward the present rulers, the Transitional National Council (TNC), is one of skepticism and ambivalence. No one knows where developments of the 'Arab Spring,' including those in Libya, will lead. North African Islamic political culture is different from that of the Middle East. In the past, Libya was characterized by a strong nationalism and moderate Islamism. That is, however, no guarantee for the future.

"Through overseas representatives, the World Organization of Libyan Jews in Or Yehuda, Israel has had some contact with the TNC. Presently, the country is only at the beginning of putting its house in order. There is tribal rivalry, many militias retain their weapons, no national army exists, and there is thus no law and order. Furthermore, there are no political parties and no civil society. It will take a long time before a Libyan constitution can be formulated and promulgated. Hopefully that would give minorities a respectful status in the country.

"The attitude of the future Libyan government toward Libyan Jews abroad will largely depend on its composition. It is far too early to assess what the role of the Islamists will be, or that of the revolutionary elite. Libya, as a Muslim country, cannot ignore the geopolitical situation in the Middle East, including the Palestinian issue.

"Psychologist David Gerbi is the one Libyan Jew who has tried to play an active role in this situation. He was born in Libya in 1955 and became a refugee after the 1967 war. He was then airlifted to Italy like many other Jews. The Libyan Jewish community, which goes back 2,500 years, ceased to exist when Gerbi brought his aunt, Libya's last Jew, to Rome in 2003. For many years he has been in favor of building bridges with the Arabs. Gerbi visited the country again in 2007 and in 2011, he went there trying to give humanitarian help to victims of the revolution in hospitals.

"When in Libya, Gerbi tried to visit former synagogues and find former cemeteries. Many had been deliberately destroyed under the Qaddafi regime. Gerbi tried to tear down a wall that prevented the entrance to ruins of a synagogue in Tripoli, but one of the militias stopped him. Gerbi has become disillusioned as he was mistreated first by Qaddafi followers and afterwards by the TNC—to the point of endangering his life. Gerbi now realizes that the TNC leadership is duplicitous and ambivalent in their attitude toward Jews.

"Gerbi's timing was wrong. He should have waited until the dust had settled and then begin what he did. A Jew who comes to restore Jewish heritage in a country undergoing a revolution is the last thing that the TNC wanted to have on its hands."

Roumani concludes: "There may still be some sympathy left for Jews among elder Libyans. As far as Libyan Jews are concerned, the new government's attitude toward the compensation issue will be a crucial test case. If compensation is paid for collective and private communal property and if synagogues can be restored, maybe Libyan Jews—at least those living outside of Israel—may pay occasional visits to the country."

Egyptian Anti-Semitism
from Mubarak to Morsi

*Z*VI MAZEL was Israeli ambassador to Egypt from 1996–2001. He also served as ambassador in Romania and Sweden. He is now a fellow of the Jerusalem Center for Public Affairs monitoring Arab issues.

"Anti-Semitism and what might be called anti-Israelism have intermingled in Egypt for many decades. Attacks on Israel often use the most depraved anti-Semitic clichés. Israel and the Jewish people are also attacked separately, even though many Egyptians consider Israel and the Jews as one and the same.

"These hate phenomena continue to flourish now as they did under Mubarak, who was president of Egypt from 1981 until 2011. To understand how the massive demonization of Israel and the Jews is structured, one has to analyze the much longer previous period."

Mazel says: "One occasion when targeting of all Jews came to light internationally was during the historic visit of Pope John Paul II to Egypt in 2000. The government-owned English language daily *The Egyptian Gazette* published a front-page editorial titled: 'Who Needs an Apology?' It referred to the absolution of the Jews by the Vatican for the murder of

Jesus. According to Editor-in-Chief Ali Ibrahim, this absolution erased all of the history, prayers and rituals, of two thousand years of Christianity. He inferred that the United States had pressured the Vatican to absolve the Jews in order to strengthen Israel.

"Under Mubarak, there was a great deal of state ownership of the media and other papers were severely censored. It was forbidden to criticize the president, the armed forces and the treatment of the Coptic minority. It was, however, permissible to attack and defame Israel and the Jews relentlessly. Islamic newspapers took their cue from the official line and their messages of Israel-hatred and anti-Semitism were vitriolic.

"Jews are mainly represented in cartoons wearing black coats and hats with large hook noses and forelocks. They were often shown slaughtering Palestinians or stabbing doves of peace. On many occasions, Jews are presented as thieves and liars. They are routinely called 'sons of monkeys and pigs.' In 1997, the weekly *Rose al Yussef* published a study that was presented for discussion at the Arab Association for Social Sciences. It determined from 'sources' of uncertain origin that Jews are perceived in Egypt as 'repulsive,' 'speaking in nasal tones,' and 'dishonest.'

"Another important hate theme is the presentation of Jews as the root of all evil and a threat to global peace. Such articles are often based on *The Protocols of the Elders of Zion*, blood libels, or even texts from the Talmud. Much respect was given to prominent French Holocaust denier Roger Garaudy who died in 2012. The initiative taken by then-Swedish Prime Minister Gunnar Persson to hold an international conference on Holocaust education in 2000 was forcefully denounced in Egypt. These are just a few examples among many.

"The rise to power in Egypt by the Muslim Brotherhood brings to the fore a movement in which Jew-hate is inherent. This organization was founded in 1928 in Egypt by a school teacher, Hassan Al-Banna, as a Pan-Islamic Movement. It developed a Muslim version of Nazi anti-Semitism.

It saw to it that Hitler's *Mein Kampf* was translated into Arabic under the title *My Jihad*. Other Nazi anti-Semitic publications were also translated. Cartoons found in the Nazi hate paper *Der Stuermer* were changed to present the Jews as the satanic enemy of Allah rather than of the German people. Writer and theorist Sayyid Qutb was a leading authority of the Egyptian Muslim Brotherhood in the 1950s and 1960s. In his popular anti-Semitic book *My Battle with the Jews*, he claimed that Jews infiltrated and corrupted Islam.

"Anti-Semitism in the post-Mubarak transition period and under President Mohammed Morsi expresses itself to a large extent in the applications of anti-Semitic motives against Israel. Israeli Prime Minister Benjamin Netanyahu continues to be shown as Hitler in the Egyptian media. A video from a mosque in October 2012 showed Egyptian President Mohamed Morsi saying 'Amen' to the prayers by an imam calling on Allah to 'destroy the Jews and their supporters.'

"One much-publicized incident in August 2012 where anti-Israelism and anti-Semitism mixed openly occurred on an Egyptian TV program similar to *Candid Camera*. The show invited popular actor Ayman Kandeel, telling him that he would appear on German TV. When the show went live, the Egyptian interviewer falsely claimed that she was an Israeli interviewing him for Israeli TV. The actor knocked her against the wall, slapped her, and cursed her. The actress Al-Beblawi, on whom the same prank was played, said on air, 'Allah did not curse the worm and the moth as much as he cursed the Jews.'"

Mazel concludes: "The mixture of anti-Semitism and anti-Israelism has become embedded in the Egyptian psyche. The Jews and the Jewish state are seen as enemies of Egypt, even though there is peace between Israel and Egypt. The rise to power of the Muslim Brotherhood, with its ideological hatred of Jews, has worsened the situation and could threaten the peace between the two countries."

Notes

1   Manfred Gerstenfeld, interview with Hans Jansen, "The Historical Roots of the Anti-Israel Positions of Liberal Protestant Churches," *Post-Holocaust and Anti-Semitism*, 57, June 1, 2007.

2   "Krise verschafft Rechtsextremisten Aufwind," *Die Welt*, October 19, 2012. [German]

3   Rachel Hirshfeld, "Neo-Nazi Party Welcomed into European Anti-Discrimination Body," *Israel National News*, July 10, 2012.

4   Manfred Gerstenfeld, "The Toulouse Murders," *Journal for the Study of Anti-Semitism*, Volume 4, 1, 2012, 165-180.

5   Eirik Eiglad, *The Anti-Jewish Riots in Oslo*, (Oslo: Communalism, 2010).

6   Cnaan Liphshiz, "In Scandinavia, kipah becomes a symbol of defiance for Malmo's Jews," *JTA*, September 24, 2012.

7   "In Malmo, record number of hate crimes complaints but no convictions," *JTA*, January 9, 2013.

8   "Israeli envoy warns against wearing skullcaps in Copenhagen," *The Times of Israel*, December 13, 2012.

9   Hannes Gamillscheg, "Dänemark: Juden fühlen sich unter Druck," *Die Presse*, January 1, 2013. [German]

10 fra.europa.eu/fraWebsite/material/.../AS-WorkingDefinition-draft.pdf.

11 library.fes.de/pdf-files/do/07908-20110311.pdf.

12 "2012 Top Ten Anti-Semitic/Anti-Israeli Slurs," Simon Wiesenthal Center.

13 Yoni Hirsch and Ilan Gattegno, "Netanyahu announces 'digital Iron Dome' to battle cyberattacks," *Israel Hayom*, October 14, 2012.

14 "Netanyahu: We're building a digital Iron Dome," *The Jerusalem Post*, January 1, 2013.

15 The Universal Declaration of Human Rights. December 10, 1948. United Nations, retrieved from www.un.org/en/documents/udhr/index.shtml.

16 The Cairo Declaration of Human Rights in Islam. Organisation of Islamic Cooperation, retrieved from www.oic-oci.org/english/article/human.htm.

17 Turan Kayaoğlu, "It's Time to Revise The Cairo Declaration of Human Rights in Islam," *Brookings*, April 23, 2012.

18 Manfred Gerstenfeld, *The Abuse of Holocaust Memory: Distortions and Responses*, (Jerusalem: Jerusalem Center for Public Affairs, 2009) 101-115. Second edition available at: http://jcpa.org/book/the-abuse-of-holocaust -memory-distortions-and-responses/

19 Miranda McGonagall, "Store and Willoch get their credit dues for endorsing Gaza book. Western double standards exposed," *Norway, Israel, and the Jews*, October 26, 2011.

20 Manfred Gerstenfeld, interview with Richard Landes, "The Muhammad Al-Dura Blood Libel: A Case Analysis," *Post-Holocaust and Anti-Semitism*, 74, November 2, 2008.

21 www.youtube.com/watch?v=mkizDpl7x_E (part 1) (viewed June 2, 2009); www.youtube.com/watch?v=369WqEJ6ChA (part 2) (viewed June 2, 2009).

22 Nadav Shragai, The *"Al-Aksa is in Danger" Libel: The History of a Lie*, (Jerusalem: Jerusalem Center for Public Affairs, 2012).

23 Günther Grass, "Was gesagt werden muss," *Suddeutsche.de*, April 10, 2012. [German]

24 "Passover suicide bombing at Park Hotel in Netanya," *Israel Ministry of Foreign Affairs*, March 27, 2002.

25 "Backgrounder: A Study in Palestinian Duplicity and Media Indifference,"

CAMERA, August 1, 2002.

26 Ethical Fallacies, University of Texas, http://projects.uwc.utexas.edu/handouts/?q=node/3

27 Manfred Gerstenfeld, "*Bin Laden versus Yassin*," Ynet, May 3, 2011.

28 Manfred Gerstenfeld, *Behind the Humanitarian Mask*, (Jerusalem: Jerusalem Center for Public Affairs and Friends of Simon Wiesenthal Center for Holocaust Studies, 2008), 22–23.

29 Dore Gold, "From 'Occupied territories' to 'Disputed territories'," *Jerusalem Letter/Viewpoints* 470, January 16, 2002.

30 "Morsi answers amen to imam's prayers for destruction of Jews," *JTA*, October 22, 2012.

31 Juliana Menasce Horowitz, "Declining Support for bin Laden and Suicide Bombing," *PewResearch Global Attitudes Project*, September 10, 2009.

32 Manfred Gerstenfeld and Tamas Berzi, "The Gaza War and the New Outburst of Anti-Semitism," *Post-Holocaust and Anti-Semitism*, 79, April 1, 2009.

33 "By the numbers: Syria deaths," CNN, January 9, 2013.

34 Ibid.

35 Manfred Gerstenfeld, Academics Against Israel and the Jews, (Jerusalem: Jerusalem Center for Public Affairs, 2007). The second edition can be read for free at: http://jcpa.org/book/academics-against-israel-and-the-jews/.

36 www.ngo-monitor.org/.

37 Ronnie Fraser, "Trade Union and Other Boycotts of Israel in Great Britain and Ireland," *Post-Holocaust and Anti-Semitism*, 76, December 1, 2008.

38 Hillel C. Neuer, "The Struggle against Anti-Israel Bias at the UN Commission on Human Rights," *Post-Holocaust and Anti-Semitism*, 40, January 1, 2006.

39 Manfred Gerstenfeld, interview with Dore Gold, "Europe's Consistent Anti-Israeli Bias at the United Nations," *Post-Holocaust and Anti-Semitism*, 34, July 1, 2005.

40 Manfred Gerstenfeld, interview with Shimon Samuels, "Anti-Semitism and Jewish Defense at the United Nations World Summit on Sustainable Develop-

ment, 2002 Johannesburg, South Africa," *Post-Holocaust and Anti-Semitism*, 6, March 2, 2003.

41 Manfred Gerstenfeld, "Anti-Semitism and Anti-Israelism in Western Schools," *Post-Holocaust and Anti-Semitism*, 112, November 1, 2011.

Acknowledgments

Many thanks are due to the Simon Wiesenthal Center for generously supporting the realization of this book.

I am grateful to Leah Horton for reviewing the initial English version and typing the book's texts. I also want to thank Wendy Cohen-Wierda for her assistance with a number of the interviews.

Most of all, I am grateful to the many interviewees who graciously shared their thoughts and expertise with me.

Several of the interviews in this book have been updated from longer versions published earlier by the Jerusalem Center for Public Affairs or in my 2010 book in Dutch, *Het Verval, Joden in een Stuurloos Nederland* (The Decay: Jews in a Rudderless Netherlands).

Books by the Same Author

Revaluing Italy, with Lorenzo Necci (Italian), 1992.

Environment and Confusion: An Introduction to a Messy Subject, 1993.

Israel's New Future – Interviews, 1994.

The State as a Business: Do-It-Yourself Political Forecasting (Italian), 1994.

Judaism, Environmentalism, and the Environment, 1998.

The Environment in the Jewish Tradition: A Sustainable World (Hebrew), 2002.

Europe's Crumbling Myths: The Post-Holocaust Origins of Today's Anti-Semitism, 2003.

American Jewry's Challenge: Conversations Confronting the Twenty-First Century, 2004.

Israel and Europe: An Expanding Abyss?, 2005.

European-Israeli Relations: Between Confusion and Change?, 2006

The Abuse of Holocaust Memory: Distortions and Responses, 2009.

Anti-Semitism in Norway (Norwegian), 2010.

American Jewry's Comfort Level: Present and Future, with Steven Bayme, 2010.

The Decay: Jews in a Rudderless Netherlands (Dutch), 2010.

Judging the Netherlands: The Renewed Holocaust Restitution Process, 1997-2000, 2011.

Books Edited:

The New Clothes of European Anti-Semitism, with Shmuel Trigano (French), 2004.

Academics against Israel and the Jews, 2007.

Israel at the Polls 2006, with Shmuel Sandler and Jonathan Rynhold, 2008.

Behind the Humanitarian Mask: The Nordic Countries, Israel, and the Jews, 2008.

Israel at the Polls 2009, with Shmuel Sandler and Hillel Frisch, 2008.

Monograph:

The Autumn 2005 Riots in France: Their Possible Impact on Israel and the Jews, 2006.

Lightning Source UK Ltd.
Milton Keynes UK
UKOW031846150713

213846UK00018B/1671/P